all were
BORN
NAKED

all were
BORN
NAKED

NO SKILLS
NO TALENTS
NO INTELLECTUAL
GIFTS

by

John Larsson

ISBN: 1-58721-234-X

Authorhouse – Rev. 6/22/06

CONTENTS

ROOTED IN MANY MYTHS IS A GRAIN OF TRUTH THAT MAKES THEM EASIER TO BELIEVE

Nothing is so firmly believed as what we least know. . .
Michel Eyquem de Montaigne

It would be helpful before you undertake the reading of this book to make a bold-spirited attempt to clear your mind of any preconceived notions or fixed beliefs about the roots of human behavior or talent. And, fret not that it may concern your personal viability, that of friends or relations, business affairs, love-making or any other aspect of life. I realize this may be easier said than done; but, if you will make this noble effort, I promise it will be well worth your while and may help you in reaching your own personal reality.

I am not out to gain wholehearted support for or against anyone or anything. I accept you as you are without any qualification as a unique, one-of-a-kind human being, matchless in mind and body and spirit to any other human individual on our planet Earth. There is no male or female distinction in my investigations or philosophic position. And, the male and female pronoun or reference in every case, when used, is automatically interchangeable. (Though I do clearly acknowledge that there are marked differences between the two.)

When I suggest some ideas or techniques that some people have sworn by and may have pursued successfully, as from any well-spread smorgasbord table, select those that appear tasty or relevant to your needs and pass over any that seem they are not.

Journalists and some of the scientists who feed society's hunger for 'scientific revelations' and serve the appetites of the listening and reading public have been winning audiences of much greater magnitude than they deserve. Good news of any kind gets delivered early and often erroneously from the fields of science. Achievements or pronouncements voiced or printed, whether actually notable or not, induce wonder in us. In their desperate hope of delivering news that people desire, they keep us in awe before the many mysteries of our lives and the mysteries of the universe. But this cannot transcend the common truths that really exist in all of our lives, or provide the answers for the myriad of insoluable biological puzzles around us. In a world in which I've got my facts and you've got yours, how can anyone discern what's really plausible?

It is not the purpose of this book to air the many shortcomings of current scientific knowledge, or to point out all of the biological questions that have been left unanswered. It is simply to strip the ambiguity from the conclusions of the hope-it-to-bes and would-like-it-to-bes. It will reveal the unvarnished, true nature of the human behaviors demonstrated often in our own daily lives and in the lives of those around us.

You will recognize, of course, that it does seem to be the cyberspace society's fashion today to absolve people of any responsibility for their own behavior. They look sympathetically upon the actions of so-called drug, alcohol and smoking addicts (habitual patterns of chosen behavior) who drive themselves into disease and death. Then we pity and excuse deviates who divide themselves from normal society, gormandizers who eat themselves into bad health and deformation. And, they continue to do this despite thoughtful, caring, professional, or spiritual advice and admonition.

Then there is the skirmish between competing scientific claims. How can anyone assume that crimes, murders, and rapes are socially or biologically driven? Or, that all behavior is in some way 'caused?' And, if so, assume that individuals do not have personal responsibility for their actions? Is it to say that we may have no control over our inappropriate or bad behaviors and that something in our bodies makes us do it?

There are people who become enslaved by an 'addiction.' Now there is nothing odd or peculiar about blaming others or one's own body for one's own conduct. That is clearly denial and the core of personal and scientific distraction.

What of the many people who have wished an end to their behavior or habit? Did so and changed. . .altered their lifestyle for a better, healthier, and more socially acceptable mode of living. What of those who have set a goal for themselves, and labored away endlessly until they made it happen? There are personal choices for good behaviors as well as the bad.

Scholarly achievement, vocational or technical achievement, outstanding physical skills, and the pure acts of loving and praying and courage are the formed choices of a free-will and moral attitude. Drug addicts, alcoholics, and smokers can and often quit on their own when they learn of the consequences of their habit. The societal disgraced or criminals can, and often have, become virtuous and responsible by personal choice.

The dawning of the manner in which you, personally, are now behaving or performing can be uncovered in a search and recollection of your fading past. If its first appearance cannot be tracked to conditions and events near your birth or soon thereafter, the influence, the spur, the learning opportunity, or the source of your behavior or lot in life will certainly pop up somewhere along your own life's path.

Several noted geneticists and molecular biologists, they who are committed to the narrow study of DNA molecules and segments of those molecules which are called genes, declared at an annual meeting of the American Association for the Advancement of Science (AAAS) that there is no such thing as a behavior gene or an intelligence gene. They spoke out in concert that, "...there is no scientific basis for any claim linking human genetics to behavior or intelligence." And, that "...efforts to link genetics to specific human behavior have come from psychologists, psychiatrists, and sociologists who have little, if any, understanding of genetics."

Incidentally, genetics remains a very specialized subject that only a very selective group in or out of the sciences are equipped to evaluate, in spite of a flood of reports concerning genetics in the media from the fields of psychology, psychiatry, medicine, education, and the social sciences.

In this year of 2000 leaders of the government Human Genome Project (HGP) and J. Craig Venter, president of Celera Genomics, Inc., a biotechnology company, have announced completion of "working draft" reference DNA sequence of the human genome. You wouldn't know it from the press

3

conferences, but scientists are still far from deciphering the human genome.

Agreeing that some of the work on this project has been overstated, computer scientist Peter D. Karp of SRI Internationale in Menlo Park, California, and in Science News, "Genome annotation is a lot like passing a piano through a nine-inch hole. It's very difficult, and it isn't immediately obvious how such a task can be accomplished." 'Annotation' or as it is now termed 'bioinformatics' is the process of making sense out of the data from the DNA sequencing, and could be the most difficult part of the projects.

Bioinformatician Sylvia J. Spengler of Lawrence Berkeley National Laboratory in California said in Science News that without successful annotation the billions of bases of DNA sequenced are essentially useless. In order to make sense out of the masses of data acquired in the past 10 years from scientists here around the world, J. Craig Venter of Celera predicted that it will take most of this century to analyze all the data. He said in Science News, "Scientists will have to invent ever-more-powerful computer algorithms to deal and understand the data.

The future is an exciting and inviting universe. If this material in any way will help you and yours along the road, and paradoxically clarify some cumbersome presumptions, it will have achieved its purpose. First, you must trust that all things and all bytes of information are not unfailingly exactly as they are publicly disclosed to us; that God helps those who help themselves; that we are each undeniably accountable for our own behavior; and our only gifts in life are the opportunities bestowed upon us.

The chapters that follow will confirm this message each in its own way. Beginning when the seeds of knowledge and skills, and the rootings of behavior and character are first slowly but clearly being formed in childhood. Where the rootings lie in those singled out in the past as being very special in their fields. Then there are various techniques, courses of habit, and disciplines that have been used by many people to reach their special state in life. Also, there can be some cause when all does not go well in one's life. The following chapters will ferret out

4

much of the reality in the world surrounding you and me.

TWEEDLEDUM AND TWEEDLEDEE

'Tis education forms the common mind, just as the twig is bent, the tree's inclin'd.

Alexander Pope

It is known that in the beginning, at their birth, all infants are created homogeneous. A newborn child of one family defines that of all others. In this true sense, barring an unfortunate congenital impairment, trauma, or developmental disability, one child is in no way singular or different in mind and behavior from any other child in the world. Nonidentical only in the biparental physical characteristics in the genetic formation of body, bone and muscle.

There is an unbroken law for the growth and development of any child. A slow step-by-step pattern of progress and training. Walking on two feet is so typically human that one might expect that it just happens. Actually there must be a considerable amount of preparation before a child can take its first step. When born it does not even have control of its head and neck muscles, and the head remains where it is placed usually about eight weeks. It is only then that it can lie on its stomach and lift its head looking straight ahead. And, normally it will be six or seven months before it can even sit upright for any length of time.

Every child at first can make only unintelligible sounds. First cooing and babbling, a definite word of any kind does not come out of it until it is about one year old, unconsciously or consciously copying the sounds and actions of its parents or siblings. It will not begin to combine words until it is about one and one-half, and will not form a grammatical sentence until two or three years of age. . .regardless of the impatience of its caregivers.

An infant only learns to recognize faces some time around the middle of its first year. And, about the age of two, can usually stand to be with other children. As unlikely as such a thing could happen, should any infant be left entirely to its own resources. . .for example, be raised among wild animals isolated from any human guidance. . .it would be unable to interrelate with other humans in the most simple ways. In other words, it would be stupid, incognizant, and unable to cope or communicate within its normal world. It could not *behave* within the conditions and restraints among its own kind. Every child is entirely dependent upon its parents or other caregivers for its mental and behavioral and cultural development.

From the reports from the news media today, it would appear that they are discovering an awful lot of different kinds of 'genes' for every human act and condition. Recognizing, of course, that most often the scientist doesn't know what the gene does (aside of making a protein), and sometimes they can't identify the gene specifically but only a 'region of interest' on the chromosome where the gene could reside. . .locating the haystack but not the needle.

Much of what we have heard reported about human genesis and maturation from the media and from many in that broad world called 'science' or 'scientists' is actually more conjectural than documented. You must understand that those whom we call 'scientists' in the all-embracing sense, each works within a very narrow field of expertise. Stepping out of the narrow field in which they were educated and now labor, they are not very much more knowledgeable nor experienced than you or I. But, they will and do speculate on reported findings for applications in other fields as do you and I. And, will attempt to suggest some drift and some role in their own fields.

Molecular biologists have made impressive strides in gaining a better understanding of the succession and growth in human physical development, and in identifying genetic sources for some diseases. They have drawn a flood of important evidence from their studies, but their findings or reports have often been either ignored or turned upside down to serve the raison d'etre of many in the fields of psychology, psychiatry, education, and social studies.

There are many who would hold themselves and others like them blameless for anomalistic behaviors with the plea that they were victims of their genetic origins. Attempts are made to absolve people of the responsibility for their own behavior. But, important contradictory evidence and logical reasoning explains that free will formed choices, conditions experienced, and environmental causes have played the pivotal role.

Considered dispassionately and reasonably, we can only blame or credit the social or cultural influences, associations with others of their kind, or environmental pressures for the whole range of individuality. That includes the span from intelligence to ignorance, the moral conscientiousness to the moral deviate. It was not a biological cause that brought about any incidence of homosexuality, immorality, abuse, criminality, or even exceptional intelligence. Free will allows us to choose those things that are life-fulfilling as well as those things which are life-impairing. We are each solely responsible for our decisions and conduct, and the choices we make in our lives. And, society can only hold its fabric together by selection out of the broad range of human behaviors those that it will approve or acclaim, some it will accept or tolerate, and others it dislikes and must condemn.

Certain behavior will be typical for every child. Every normal boy and girl will pass each stage in development at somewhat different times and at different rates of speed. . .but this is in no way a measure of intelligence. Children will change at varying times in their lives, they learn and grow depending upon the associations and events they experience and upon their environment. Findings of studies of the mental growth of infants have been repeated so sufficiently often that it is well established that intelligence testing in the first few years of an infant's life will have no predictive validity.

Study after study has revealed that any attempt to evaluate children in the early years has no value in judging preschool or school age intelligence or behavior. Up to four or five years of age, measures by the standards of IQ testing are of no use in predicting a child's cognitive skills later in life. IQ testing methods use problem solving techniques normally exposed in an academic environment. Many people with high IQs are limited in practical and common sense matters. And, all of these findings in toto are not in dispute among the psychometricians.

9

Notice how helpless and undeveloped in both mind and body a human newborn infant is upon entering this world compared to those in the animal kingdom. A good example would be the stray cats who have made their home in the large marsh behind our home. From whence they came does not matter, but they have been there existing wild in our marsh winter and summer for quite a long time. We often put out commercial cat food to supplement the mice, shrews, and other small creatures that they catch in the marsh for their regular meals. . .which is also to our advantage, of course.

During their residence there, a small litter of young have appeared upon occasion. One of the cats would disappear for a time, then reappear for food, and soon would arrive at the food bowl at our door with a tiny kitten or so. Though at first only tottering about, it was only a matter of weeks before the kittens could be seen stalking through the marsh hunting down their own meals biologically driven. . .but not so with human infants.

How long and devious is the time of preparation for the sons and daughters of we humans before they are able to feed themselves, earn and produce their own meals, or survive on their own. So long a period of time must pass in attending to every simple need, protecting, advising, supporting as well as training and educating them so they will become normal, society-acceptable humans. Though they are each outfitted with a much greater brain size and capacity than that of the animals who can fend for themselves almost from the time of their birth.

Though human infants are born into the world in a state of helplessness, of course, within the first four years their brains will have masterminded a host of amazingly complicated neural connections. . .motor coordination, the retention of memories, the acquisition of a vocabulary, and the ability to develop patterns of thought. External stimuli, environment, and outside influences bring about most of these brain-building processes.

Behavior and brain development comes to them by learning, experiencing, and, most importantly, their manner of living by the transmission of a culture from generation to generation beginning as soon as the primary caregivers take over. This is critically important regardless whether the child's skin is white or black or yellow. . .without regard to nationality or environs or most anything else since culture leaves an indelible mark on behavior.

During the first years of life a child is a veritable learning machine. . .testing new motions and actions of its body, listening to new sounds, feeling many new sensations, and forming patterns of behavior. Differing amounts of their progress in behavior or skills or intelligence will correspond directly to the nature and the quality of their early learning opportunities whether good or bad.

Unfortunately, with a flip of a coin fate will decide upon an infant's environment, whether born into affluence or poverty, with or without a lustrous heritage, with the blessing of nurturing caregivers or the curse of abuse. It cannot decide how tall it will grow; there is very little it can do about its looks; it is not able to choose its parents nor the period in history in which it is to be born.

However, many children will overcome, thrive and fare well in a variety of environments and situations, disadvantaged or not. Also, as a result of some changes in the circumstances throughout each life, stupid people can sometimes become bright, apathetic people alert, weak and wasting people lively and strong, poor people rich and famous, and demoralized people virtuous because of discipline, changes in associations, special therapy or simply dumb luck.

Note that slow or arrested physical development can be the result of infectious disease or physical, psychological, and social traumas not necessarily inherited. However, geneticists reasonably expect that their efforts in the study of the influence of genes may also someday lead them to predicting predispositions of developing some of these conditions or diseases and finding the means of combating them. As of today genetic treatments have cured no one, but have caused some deaths.

Even when living within the same family, each child is subject to nonidentical influences that will affect each child differently both mentally and physically and in behavior. Because of these nonidentical influences, nonidentical experiences, every human behavior will be found spread evenly across all social classes, among college or high school educated or dropouts, rich or poor. . .all economic levels. Parents are often amazed how the behavior or development of each of their children will sometimes spring so very differently from the same parents and parenting style. Siblings, even identical twins, raised in the same environment may eventually make very different choices.

Infants begin life with a certain number of built-in responses in order to ensure survival; but the most distinguishing nature of human behavior is that so much must be first experienced and learned, and very little acquired innately. Animal behavior, on the other hand, is governed by pre-programmed patterns and by built-in immediate and automatic responses to environmental stimuli. Human behavior depends upon new learning experiences and associations, and memories of experiences past, and does not respond automatically to any given stimulus. Thus, there is a clear distinction between animal and human behavior.

Environment, effectual caregivers, learning opportunities and experience have decided the lives of the exceptional achievers in the past. The greatest of the writers, artists, composers, and others who have been immortalized in history did not gain their skills innately. They had to learn their crafts, gain their knowledge and were nurtured, grounded, and coached by teachers and others who had gone before them. Their biographies show that as novitiates they did not discover their own unique voice in their chosen or focused interest. They were unable to or did not have the courage to react against their training to form their own individual style and direction. But, after they had been enriched by the experiences in their lives and trained, educated, and bolstered by their performances, they were finally able to scale to great heights in their chosen fields.

Our minds retain a near perfect record of everything that passes before us. And, because each person lives in a unique environment shaped by nonidentical circumstances and relationships, each has a particular and special array of chosen and accidental experiences. Because of the exclusively intimate and unipersonal experiences in each life, each individual becomes his or her own kind of person like no other on the face of the earth. *And surely, in the beginning, other than physical constraints, we are all born on an equal plane with the Einsteins, Rembrandts, Shakespeares, Michael Jordans, Jimmy Connors, et al.*

The disposition of curiosity is something so unequal in people. In the germination of curiosity about something. . .in the nurturing of interest or excitement about some subject or activity or behavior. . .we respond positively to encouragement and recognition. People react credulously to praise. As they strive toward some vision they have for themselves, there is a hunger for any assurance that their small victories are recognized as progress toward some greater purpose.

When basking in praise, a person can be vulnerable to a type of behavior that is encouraged by someone else. In associations with others, a common practice or behavior can be acquired and seem correct. Attentiveness to 'that's the way it's done around here' leads to assurance that what someone else is attempting to grasp for themselves. . .is right. This is a kind of influence that can appear in almost anyone's behavior and achievement pattern.

Sometimes special skills or knowledge or a behavior path can be hidden in a person's past, and go unnoticed until it is eventually revealed. We can be surprised by special ability or knowledge or a particular behavior when it comes from a person whom we would consider as having no background or interest in such a quality or activity. Sometimes a person who seemed to have no aptitude or interest or proficiency in something, suddenly will display a surprising, remarkable competence, awareness, inclination, or know-how when called upon. It is clear in such a case, of course, that there must have been a good amount of experience, trial, or study somewhere in that person's past not revealed before. No kernel of knowledge, no special skill, and no special behavior is formed or developed out of thin air. There must be some coaching or experiencing in their background at some time somewhere.

There are so many boggling conditions, influences, forces, and processes in our lives over which we have no control, and so many things that affect our fortunes or failures that seem to come with the roll of the dice. *Is it little wonder that we are misled to believe that our fate or that of our children is to be ordained by some predestining force in our 'genes,' or by some inherent 'gift' or spiritual power?*

To be of notice or make an uncommon mark in any way in this world of ours a person must undergo a prolonged and severely disciplined training with a spirited and impressive influence from someone or something. Special behavior or achievement will never happen by chance. The influence or discipline is usually spurred by caregivers or the efforts of others with a forcible personal interest in an impressive child or a submissive adult.

We humans can profit from our life's experiences; and, whenever it is revealed to us, we can profit from the wisdom or the folly of those who have lived before us. Human beings are not predetermined automatons. They cannot be intellectually dissected or categorized. It is impossible to predict what a given person will do or accomplish. However, this will probably not discourage any psychologists, psychiatrists, or sociologists from trying.

My research and approach to the subject of behavior and its path, as it deals with such broad, complex, and personal subjects as intelligence, achievement, and deviate or socially incorrect behaviors, can be expected to be challenged by someone. *However, all of the information and research explored here cannot be proven untrue. There is no science to deny these premises or their validity.*

MIND GAMES THAT PEOPLE PLAY

"We come to the inescapable conclusion that human addiction is largely a product of the mind, not the body."
Michael S. Gazzaniga
President of the Cognitive Neuroscience Institute

According to a quip by Samuel Butler, the English writer, "A hen is only an egg's way of making another egg." A normalcy in life is often interpreted counterfactually to explain a person's particular conviction. As is this counter-critical comment by Tallulah Bankhead, noted actress and film star of the 30s and 40s, "Cocaine habit-forming? Of course not. I ought to know. I've been using it for years."

There are many human frailties woven into that collective conscious and unconscious neural processing that we call the 'mind' that direct and influence our behavior. 'Denial' is a person's refusal to acknowledge or recognize the existence or reality of something. Refusal to accept accountability or responsibility for a limitless range of bad behavior.

The conventional wisdom regarding addiction to nicotine and drugs is that something inside of one's self takes control when one uses the substance. The nicotine 'addicted' are forced to continue to smoke tobacco even though they really desire not to. *This assumption continues to persist despite the fact that not long ago, as was the fashion at that time, almost all of our friends and associates smoked cigarettes. Today I rarely meet or know anyone who does. And, they who quit smoking did so voluntarily without the aid of therapy or a counteractive agent of any kind.*

Statistics show that about 82 percent of adults in the United States use alcohol in some form, yet its abuse rate is estimated at less than 6 percent. According to the National Household Survey (NHS), 77 million Americans have experimented with illicit drugs at some time in their life. But, drug abuse along with alcohol abuse is only about 10 percent of the adult population.

Because of concerns over the widespread use of narcotics among soldiers during the Vietnam war, President Richard Nixon ordered a large scale study on the veterans returning home. Dr. Lee Robbins of Washington University in St. Louis, Missouri, was appointed to conduct the study. From the 13,760 soldiers returning home during 1971, she selected 1,400 who tested as unquestionable drug users. Upon testing this sample group 8 to 12 months after their return home, 92 percent of those who had been using drugs quit. Simply leaving behind any dependency on the drugs used in Vietnam.

During the early part of World War II, I served as a civilian office manager at the Army Station Hospital at Fort Snelling, Minnesota. At that same time researchers from the University of Minnesota were working at the hospital testing and developing what would become the Minnesota Multiphasic Personality Inventory (MMPI). It was the common, if not misdirected, practice of the small town draft boards during World War II to purposely draft their town drunk or druggie into the service (and they all seemed to have at least one). They reasoned that the army discipline would provide a cure.

The hospital at that time had a few cells with bars that were used for patients who were difficult to control or needed isolation. Commonly these alcohol or drug abusers would arrive at the station reception center along with all other draftees. Those who became suspect as substance abusers would be transferred to the Station Hospital on the post for observation. There they were placed in the cells with no access to a substance of any kind. After a short time without any alcohol or drugs, if they exhibited some kind of withdrawal or other symptoms of substance abuse, they would be summarily discharged and returned to the draft board that had sent them there.

Because of this, the MMPI researchers had many such cases at hand for study and testing within their program. The MMPI studies on these men consistently showed that those beset with substance abuse were characterized by anxiety, depression, and other antisocial traits. This signaled, of course, the real cause of the 'addiction' of those abusers of alcohol and drugs, which could be applied also to those with nicotine dependence. The substance itself was simply a crutch to lean upon while denying and covering a more serious problem. Just a symptom or manifestation of the disease, not the disease itself. The cure, of course, would require the help of a psychoanalytically trained therapist who would regard the substance abuse as a symptom of an underlying psychological conflict. Not a need for patches nor twelve-step group programs.

Normally users of drugs, alcohol, or nicotine can control its use. They can stop such a habit or practice when shown a good reason to do so. I smoked my first cigarette, for example, when I was only seven years old. Smoking was common among my contemporaries, and cigarettes were cheap and always accessible in some way. In my early teens I began smoking a pack-a-day. Over the years, I graduated to two packs, three, and then four packs-a-day.

At a point later in our lives, my wife and I were buying one carton plus two packs of menthol cigarettes every other day. When we both finally came to realize and admit that we had a denigrating, unhealthy, life-threatening habit as well as a very expensive one, we both quit on the same day. That was thirty years ago, and we haven't used any form of tobacco since that day. There were some pangs and involuntary reaching for cigarettes for a time, but that too was soon erased.

Drugs and alcohol and the use of tobacco often provide something to lean or rely upon to ease anxiety in social encounters, work responsibilities, and various confrontations. The majority of substance *abusers* have some diagnosable personality disorder. There are many who can only function when on their substance of choice. It has been shown that when the substance is clinically removed and any physiological dependence on it is no longer a factor, hard core compulsive substance users will still return to their habit. Their bodies don't crave the substance. . .their minds do. And, mind problems, psychologically driven cravings, are difficult to cure.

Mind problems, chronic misconceptions, dog us every day. Why should a cloud of confusion surround the debates over the reasons why there are gays or lesbians, and their 'civil rights.' Throughout nature the role of the male and female has been clearly defined. Without challenge its purpose is for reproduction and survival of the classes and divisions of nature, the fauna and flora of every region, time, or period. This includes, of course, the survival and reproduction of the human race. Any activity aside from that purpose is just fun and games. . .sexual deviation and carnal desires. The common mistake and misunderstanding of the general public is that they choose not to serve the spirit and good of the majority in their attempts to appease an unappeasable few.

Arthur Eric Rowton, who created sculptures, engravings, and designed typography as Eric Gill, said that an artist is not a different kind of person, but every person is a different kind of artist. Much of our understanding of people can be lost in definition. A clear translation of the terminology used should clarify the confusion in public belief or sentiment touching upon kinds or classes of people when it runs counter to conditions that are simply modes of behavior.

A person who is loving and caring or someone who is immoral, or again someone who displays unusual intelligence, is not a different kind of person, but a person with a different kind of behavior. Someone who performs criminal acts, or one who performs homosexual acts is not a different kind of person, but a person who prefers or pursues a different kind of behavior. This is a behavior formed by choice, not a cultural class in society.

On the other hand, there are classes or groups of people who can be plainly separated as a class with a pronounced, common difference because of race, religion, nationality, a common culture, gender, etc. Of course, you will find a complete range of behavior within each of the classes or divisions. It would be unimaginable to expect that everyone within any one of these groups or classes would behave exactly alike. The complete range of behaviors would appear within each group.

My wife and I have been close friends over the years with a couple who have identical twin sons. The father is as virile as the mother is pretty and feminine. They have another daughter and son who are as humanly normal, womanly or manly as their parents. One of the adult identical twin sons, as virile as the father, is married with children in a happy, heterosexual family.

The other twin cohabits openly with a male partner and asocial homosexual friends. Identical twins who have exactly the same genetic material. . .not behavior brought about through their genes, but a developed and chosen behavior from an environmental or indiscreet social experience. Understand, of course, when a person is sexually abused by someone in childhood (not necessarily by a parent but by some adult), it can create great confusion about sexual identity.

Then there's the mystique surrounding the cloning of sheep, rhesus monkeys, and possibly humans. Is it a concern because we are facing a dilemma of having crowds of clones who look identical? Fears of hordes of copies with identical personalities, intelligence, emotional and psychological selfsameness? Every person indistinguishable from any of the others? *Of course not!* We will not be in a world of ditto-heads. If eventually cloned, we will find how different they can be.

This really only addresses that similar product of the genetic process that happens often in the course of natural gestation. . .the identical twins. Regardless of the tales of twins separated at birth but still sharing certain similarities in functions or preferences, identical twins never have identical personalities or even brains. They can be distinguished by physical and mental traits. They develop their behavior from the time of birth as do we all, from nonidentical associations and reactions to our environment. They are each their own person.

Typical of media hype, to a public that is conditioned to believe that virtually everything seems technologically possible, is the case of Richard Seed. A man with no money, no standing with physicists, no commitment from a physician who could perform the procedure, and no couple willing to undergo it, did announce he would soon start cloning humans commercially. As a result he burst onto the national scene, became a focus of network news, frightened 19 countries into signing bans against cloning, and caused speeches and warnings from Congress and the White House. Most scientists in the field agreed that he had no chance of pulling off any such science-fiction cloning factory that he had proposed. Just another instance of a science crazed media turning someone falsely into a scientific authority.

The federal government embarked upon the 'Human Genome Project' employing thousands of scientists and technicians around the world with Congress's authorization in 1990 to spend $3 billion over 15 years on this bold plan originally to be completed in the year 2005. Of course, also spurring the growth in private industry's entry into this genomic grand experiment by a scientist in Rockwell, Maryland, and others. And, when money is waiting to be made, you can expect some remarkable claims to surface with awesome prospects for profits, as in the proliferating commercial programs for quitting smoking.

A gene is a functional DNA segment, a stretch of DNA that specifies the composition of a protein. In turn this may affect whether and at what rate that protein combines with other proteins to form a complex human physical product. Genetic functions become a combination of a complex network of biological reactions and social and environmental relationships. Leaders of the Genome Project consistently downplay the role of genes in determining behavior.

But culture can! Each society throughout the world has its own distinct emotional, psychological, intellectual, and spiritual characteristics. Each collective body of humanity, each race, each nationality, each religious commonality with different rules of reverence for a divine power, each body politic has its own articles of faith, teachings accepted through tradition, a mode of thought or behavior that has been fossilized by a people continuously from generation to generation. And, when people with opposite or contrasting principles as to what is morally or customarily right or wrong share a community, it must result in a conflict that is probably impossible to correct.

When each ethnic or religious group is a subsociety with their own social enclaves and few institutional ties between the groups, there is a great potential for crossing swords. This is happening in Northern Ireland, among Serbs and Albanian Muslims, a constant climate in the Middle East, cause for slaughter in Africa and killings in Asia, and there seems to be no middle ground to quiet the storm of malicious, if not lethal, conflict. And, each continues to be blindly impartial to one's own group, race, religion, or politics, and is intolerant of those who differ.

In the United States, the 'melting pot' of diversity, and a multireligious, multicultural, multiracial world, there is continual discord between the blacks and whites, differing and hostile undercurrents in relationships between Protestants and Catholics, anti-Semitic undertones among contrary cultures, and disesteem for any immigrant group. And, any attempt to meld customs, beliefs, attitudes of right or wrong conduct are doomed to failure before they begin. And, a question rarely asked is "Why?" Why are blacks distrusted and feared by whites? Why are homosexuals repugnant to most everyone else? Why is there hate and distrust between those with differing religious beliefs? Why, each among their own kind, haven't they taken greater steps straightforwardly to repair their characterization among opposite groups? Complete segregation by mutual consent of the differing factions or cultures within our society (not forced integration) seems to be the only practical solution for a lasting, common peace.

In 1973 my wife and I became a part of a small group in Minnesota that organized and funded a program to bring children separated by the 'troubles' in Northern Ireland to Minnesota for a six-week holiday. With the aid of a woman in Belfast who had suggested such a program, Sarah Hughes, and a school principal from Belfast, David Russell, 120 children were carefully picked to make the trip. Half of the children ages nine, ten, and eleven, were Catholic and half Protestant. . .half boys and half girls. They were all from the besieged sections of Ulster controlled by the United Kingdom.

Each child was placed discreetly with a family of their own faith (which was not our first option but a stony demand from their parents in Northern Ireland). Each of the foster families were carefully and strictly screened. The spirit of the program was to show the children how people of different faiths and different backgrounds could live peacefully with each other, and hopefully instill in them a tolerance for other faiths and cultures. The program was overwhelmingly successful in that the children had the time of their lives, and the host families responded so very warmly and carried away fond memories. Similar programs copying that first one in Minnesota continue each summer in many cities throughout the country.

My wife and I were invited to come and spend several weeks in Northern Ireland in l977, l988, and again in l996. We have visited with families there who had been involved in the program in l973 or later on. Other than for negotiated periods to quiet the storm, these cultures persist in their separation as you may have noted in news reports recently.

An incident when the children were leaving home in l973 confirms the depth of the cultural division. One family upon presenting a parting gift to the Protestant child who had been in their care, wrote on the package "to our Irish friend."   The Protestant child rejected it angrily with the uncharitable comment, "I'm British, not Irish."   Speaking with friends in Northern Ireland, they observed that, in spite of the peace efforts and agreements, the division will never end.

Mind   problems,   counterfactual   interpretations   of information, popular faulted perceptions, and societal conflicts are just some of the sentiments and convictions that foment groups or individuals in society to perpetuate disaccord between themselves.   Mind problems foster the persuasive forces that drive people into their abnormal conduct or nonconformity.

How does a bright boy or girl, a reasonable young man or woman become an amoral deviate or calculating killer? How can anyone be led into hating society and be embittered against everything upright and innocent?   Is it because of mind problems, substance abuse, denial, or confusion about what is right and what is wrong? Or, does it spring from a fundamental spirit, the underlying sentiment of the differing beliefs, values, customs, and practices of self-exiling cultures?

Research has discovered that possibly the conflicts we have discussed or the environment may be the causal agent of some diseases.   For example, Dr. Caroline M. Tanner of the Parkinson's Institute in Sunnyvale, California, said recently in the Journal of the American Medical Association, "For the first time today we can say that for most people with Parkinson's disease diagnosed after age 50, it's most commonly caused by environmental factors." She led a study on Parkinson's patients taken from a World War II twins registry that determined environment, not genes, as the cause of most occurrences of Parkinson's disease.

The sciences have long searched for the origin of pain. There is a veritable epidemic of back pain in the United States today. Chronic back pain is second only to the common cold as a cause for lost work time. Chronic pain patients (chronic tension headache, pelvic or back pain, temporomandibular-joint disorder, keyboard operator's repetition strain injury) are a source of frustration and annoyance. Maladies doctors can neither explain nor alleviate except in recognizable aging calcification or injuries. Terrible spasms of pain can be so incapacitating and yet arise from no identifiable physical abnormality.

Take phantom-limb pain. . .after an amputation there can be a constant burning and cramping feeling exactly like the limb was still there. No nerve impulses, of course, so where does the pain originate from? Studies have pointed to mundane stuff that neither doctors nor patients like to consider. . .that the antecedents of pain lie elsewhere than in muscle, bone, or injury. Solutions for chronic pain may lie more in what goes on around one than in what is going on inside. The salient causal factors seem to be social rather than physical. This might give pause for expanding the narrow path in the studies to find genetically driven diseases to more causes lodged in personal psychology or cultural conflicts.

Could there be some oversight in not studying or treating the underlying psychogenic seat of these conditions? Craving is the essence of addiction. . .or say, obesity. Such people are quick to seize upon any excuse other than their own self-indulgence. It is true that people who are fat are so because they eat more than their bodies require. The compulsion to use drugs or alcohol despite their adverse consequences, in people who want to keep using them, possibly cannot be cured.

EACH WILL EXPLORE THE UNEXPLORED IN HIS OWN WAY

Give me a dozen healthy infants, well-formed, and my own specified world to bring them up in and I'll guarantee to take any one at random and train him to become any type of specialist I might select. . .doctor, lawyer, artist, merchant chief; and, yes, even beggarman and thief, regardless of his talents, penchants, tendencies, abilities, vocations, and the race of his ancestors.

. . .John Broadus Watson, *Behaviorist*

An astounding biological transformation takes place when a human male sperm cell joins with a female ovum. The fertilized cell divides over and over, forming brain, nervous system, arms, legs, and so on until birth when a child's anatomy is virtually complete. A child enters this world with a mass of brain cells far more immense and boundless than that of the nearest animal species. A capacity far beyond that which it would need to keep alive and live its life within its given environment, to communicate primarily with its own kind, and to reproduce itself.

At infancy a child with its first step, first word, and with its first introduction into this world, begins to accumulate the unique experiences throughout its life that will form its behavior patterns, intelligence, and personality. These behavior patterns, learned from the environment or culturally transmitted, or arising from those who will come in contact with the child and later the adult, will form an artist or writer, a doctor or athlete, a criminal or sexual deviate. Directed into ranges of influence for good or for bad, by chance or by someone's design.

The brain devotes most of its time in the early years gathering and processing material and information it is exposed to. Consciously the child will be aware of experiences and stimuli that it faces at every moment. Unconsciously the mind gathers as well experiences of vision, touch, taste, hearing, and smelling with which the conscious mind cannot or chooses not to occupy itself. The kaleidoscopic processing of all of this information and experience is constant.

The destination or future of the child is not then determined by birth gifts or inherent attributes, but by its singular experiences during its life. It is a uniqueness molded by individual environment, one-of-a-kind associations, its own separate place in the scheme of things that will dictate and motivate its behavior. That is behavior in such a broad range of moral attitudes, approach to living, preferred entertainment, fads or fashions, thrills, risktaking, or trailblazing. . .seeking novelty, conflict, challenge or passivity, apathy or detachment.

Many of us paint and sing and dance or play a guitar. Others restore cars or do needlepoint or cook wonderful dinners. We use our experience of the past and the subconscious processing within our minds to do it. We do it just as famous artists, designers, and writers have done. The only differences among us is in the way each of us explores the unexplored. What a person becomes is a person's private responsibility. . .be it a life in mediocrity, one with special skills, that of a scholar or cleric, or a humanitarian.

A 'genius' in Roman mythology was a guardian spirit that attended every person from birth to death. Our lexicographers have given it a different general definition, 'A person with extraordinary intelligence and creative powers.' The conventional wisdom is to picture this as someone with an exceptional natural capacity of intellect shown in creative and original works in art, writing, music, science, etc. . .a 'born with talent.' They disregard all of the labor and time and dedication that brought it about. As Simone de Beauvoir, the French writer said, *"One is not born a genius, one becomes a genius."*

Deep down inside everyone believes they are especially intelligent and creative, and secretly wish they were more so. Of course, we know the wonderful feeling we get when an instant awakening hits us. That inexplicable revelation we call 'inspiration.' We want to shout it out and tell the whole wide world. Everyone at some time has experienced the exhilaration that comes when they have given birth to some kind of new idea or discovery.

You will appreciate these choice words of Mark Twain, *"What is it that confers the noblest delight? What is that which swells a man's breast with pride above which any other experience can bring to him? Discovery! To know that you are walking where none others have walked; that you are beholding what human eye has not seen before; that you are breathing a virgin atmosphere. To give birth to an idea. . .to discover a great thought. . .an intellectual nugget, right under the dust of a field that many a brain-plow had gone before."*

The mind is like a flower that is bursting into blossom when its subconscious potential is realized, and you exploit its capacity for gathering and processing information. Ideas are only different combinations of the information, experiences and images fashioned in the kaleidoscopic processing within the subconscious mind interacting with our conscious mind. We then fashion new forms and fresher statements from all of the information and images accumulated from the time of our birth. The 'imagination' does not generate anything that has never been witnessed or experienced before.

The human mind is a marvelous creation with its fantastic capacity for absorbing and processing information, gaining a treasury of private knowledge for every individual. We each have this fluid and shifting 'stream of consciousness' at the borderline of unconscious thought. The fluid and shifting interaction between conscious thought and the subconscious recording and processing, and then the sifting through memories to form our own original combinations of things.

Lest we forget, knowledge alone is not wisdom. People can go to schools and gain much knowledge, but they may not have wisdom. Again wisdom is something acquired through the experiences of the individual. There is a common sense, a sense that clearly can choose what is right from what is wrong. This is learned from the wisdom and folly of contemporaries and those that have lived before us. . .experiences interacting emotionally and socially with family and friends and casual encounters that teaches correct or incorrect human relationships.

Considering the world we live in today we may wonder what happened to the discipline and smooth finish that children were given and that society expected yesterday. The world today is well-supplied with rude people spouting amoral ideology and demanding their rights. There is the confusion that surrounds attempts to find causes for various behaviors, good or bad, and people tend to accept whichever theory confirms their own presuppositions. Because issues dealing with behavior patterns and causes are of so much interest in today's society, there are specialists of all kinds presenting hypotheses for the cause and the source of all manner of conduct. The news media will continue to publish claims and counterclaims and simplistic genetic correlations whether or not they are based upon true evidence or simply faulty conjecture. Such statistical correlations aren't necessarily equivalent to causation, but can easily be mistaken for a cause or origin of a behavior or disease.

A host of personal and social circumstances affect each person's development. Acceptance of the belief that our capacities have been encoded in our genes might intimidate many people into believing it would be fruitless to pursue steps that could change or improve their position or their enjoyment of a better life. This would be completely wrong to inhibit hopes and dreams with this excuse since no skills or intelligence are spawned at birth.

Diagnostic labels such as may originate from I.Q. testing, for example, can seriously deflate or inflate a persons self-image and progress in academics, in the workplace, or in human relationships. These and similar labels can become part of a file in a growing body of data that can follow and hinder a person throughout life.

It remains, that in reaching beyond mediocrity, an individual must devote an enormous amount of time in education and trial before succeeding in any kind of endeavor. Every one of those who made a special mark in their lives fell heir only to special learning opportunities, some persuasive influence that spurred them on, and the circumstances that permitted them to dedicate every moment of their lives to their special interest.

Moreover, people also succeed in their endeavors by

exploring and exploiting the past. Studying the works of those that have gone before them and imitating their techniques and methods. This was declared, affirmed in an Old Testament quotation from 'The Book of Ecclesiastes' (the author believed to have been the wise King Solomon):

> "What has been, that will be; what has been done, that will be done. Nothing is new under the sun. Even the thing of which we say, 'See, this is new!' has already existed in the ages that preceded us."

And, we must acknowledge that, as time passes, we become more wise with our aging and experience.

DELIBERATELY WE WEAVE THE FABRIC OF OUR BEHAVIOR

Sow an act, and you reap a habit. . .Sow a habit, and you reap a character. . .Sow a character, and you reap a destiny.

Charles Reade

There is a type of bamboo plant in Asia that, from the time the seed is planted in the ground, takes five years before it will appear above the ground. During this long period of time, before any part of this plant can be seen at the surface, it is carefully spreading a complex system of roots below ground to support the tree that is to come. When the plant reaches its fifth year and breaks the surface, in a period of only six or eight weeks it raises a bole 100 feet or more toward the sky.

Human behavioral development and achievement have unmistakably well-ordered paths. There is a beginning with a compelling urge of interest often spawned by some other person's impact or pressure; followed by uninterrupted stages of self-enlightenment and self-preparation to set the root structure, a foundation of gained knowledge and mechanistic skill; it then bursts forth with recognition and acceptance by an admiring audience whoever or whatever it may be. An integration of the best or worst of what has been with the best or worst of what is unfolding today.

There are no secret passageways or shortcuts in this process. 'Inspiration' and 'imagination' are merely evidence that this process exists. There are no 'gifts' that make any accomplishment effortless. *The only gifts we receive are the opportunities we fall heir to.*

The materials for human development are gathered from two kinds of information. . .the intellectual information that results from reading, talking, and listening, and the sensory information that comes with our living experiences within chosen interests. Ernest Hemingway said about good writers, "They must learn and know as near everything as possible." Unconvincing and

31

uninteresting writing which beginners produce fails for the simple reason they have a mistaken notion that their 'imagination' can produce something out of a void. They must fill their well of knowledge and experience to the full with information within the subject or venture they have chosen to pursue.

For clarity, let's divide the functions of thought processing into two distinct and separate roles. First, the conscious mind awake and alert. . .that observable part directly aware and reacting to everything around it. Then, the unconscious mind. . .the greater part of the thought and memory processing, not observable, independently perceiving its universe and never forgetting anything that is ever experienced during a lifetime. Think of your subconscious mind as a guardian angel, always looking after you from within, dispensing subtle perceptions day and night. Streams of information and images being intertwined into new thoughts and original combinations.

The subconscious mind will bring forth information and imagery to conscious awareness from its vast personal library when there is a need for it, and without respect for morality, cultural rules, or ethics. It is here that the processing and the combining of all of the experiences and information in substratum form takes place.

Evaluations and conceptions of intelligence and inventiveness by educators are dependent upon school performance and assessment, rarely considering the influences that have contributed to or limited an individual's performance. They measure only school-related abilities in an educational environment. Many children rated extraordinary or 'gifted' at school age have never become achieving adults. And, many adults who have achieved notable works or performances were not considered exceptional as school age children.

Many methods of scoring learning potential or mastery of specific areas of knowledge have been practiced and studied with considerable disagreement within the educational community as to what intelligence really must be. Theorists in psychology have attempted to identify and sort into categories different levels or types of intelligence, absorbed in measurement rather than comprehending human nature. They agree only that some human acts and their products are intelligent, and others are not. . .that some people perform intelligently and creatively, and others do not.

Intelligence and creative strengths are too complex to be explained by simple classification. Their appearances and source seem to defy human logic or apperception. The guiding principle in this book will be that novel thinking or smarts results from long periods of activity and observation, intimate experiences within a chosen field of interest. . .or, conversely, from the lack of it.

The important achievements of history have been the result of prolonged and diligent work. We have to recognize that an extraordinary amount of time and effort goes into each great accomplishment. We may look upon a creative achievement as a remarkable and marvelous thing and overlook the extraordinary amount of self-preparation and labor that preceded it. It is the entire journey rather than the single event that rewards great achievement.

Genes produce proteins that affect our physical development, physical functions, but will not decide what we become. Genetics cannot really tell us much about our successes or failures. We are complex organisms who will lead multifarious lives. Our experiences and biological makeup will interact in unpredictable ways.

We develop special traits or the so-called 'innate talents' because of a burning desire for information or a curiosity about a particular sphere or milieu, a style of behavior, a methodology or a what-have-you inspired by someone's or something's persuasive force. That force, for good or for bad as it may be, could be a parent's direction or influence. It could be an idol, someone admired, a role model, a mentor. Or it could come from an environment one grows up within or was neighbor to that impressed one to the extent that the continued pursuit of the information about it made one, as William Shakespeare wrote, ". . .know a hawk from a handsaw." It is intense curiosity that breeds the higher levels of intelligence and inventiveness that results in special accomplishments by anyone.

What an individual is able to accomplish, of course, can depend to a critical degree on the will of Heaven at birth. Upon a rich cultural heritage, or not; devoted, skilled, professional, contributing parents, or not; supportive associations, or not; affluence or poverty; an object of racism, or gender bias, or not. Even some of those things than an individual does not control can be overcome to a certain degree, but we cannot minimize or overlook their positive or negative forces.

Some of Albert Einstein's teachers felt his intelligence was limited. He withdrew from his Munich high school at age fifteen (never liked school), then failed his examination for admission to the Zurich University (Polytechnikum). Albert appeared deficient to others due partly to dyslexia which caused him great difficulty in speech and reading. However, he spoke of a deep and lasting impression made upon him when his father made a gift to him of a compass when was only five years old. He had reacted with complete wonder at the behavior of the needle in its determination to point to magnetic north. Also, he would sit for hours on end persistently searching for solutions to mathematical puzzles given to him by his paternal uncle, Jacob, who had a very comprehensive education in mathematics, and with whom Albert kept in touch throughout his developing years. This probably was what prompted Albert to begin self-study of algebra and geometry about the age of eight, and inflamed his focus on the precision of the sciences.

Edgar Degas, the French painter and one of the impressionists who favored ballet dancers and theater scenes, no doubt was spurred unintentionally to his career choice by his father, Auguste. On Sunday mornings Auguste would pick up his son for expeditions to the Louvre in Paris and other galleries, pointing out favorite paintings and displaying his love for art. They would also visit his father's friends who owned many of the paintings of Rubens, Rembrandt, and other classical artists.

Study of the background of any exceptional display of creativity or intelligence in someone will always reveal some persuasive force, supporting milieu, or a prodding hand able to provide the information and coaching. Sometimes the coach's grounding in the subject or field is inconspicuous, and his or her contribution is overlooked. This is true as well with those who are labeled as child prodigies. Those considered 'gifted,' are said to have 'special talents,' and seem to accomplish amazing things at an unbelievable early age. (Noting, of course, many of those who were said to be prodigies as children never became accomplished virtuosi after reaching adulthood, no longer subject to the persuasive force that brought them to their earlier successes.)

Few child prodigies have developed into continuing successful adult artists. Yehudi Menuhin, violinist, after achieving great world acclaim as a child prodigy, faded from the general public scene later in his career, though he did continue as a conductor. Parents' roles in the making of child prodigies often are a pathological obsession to force and exhibit a child's training, and to keep alive a commitment to a career.

A child's first attempts at anything may not be substantially better than those of other children, but when their works are noticed and praised, and driven or spurred by the attention they receive, they become more and more interested and dedicated to follow a particular direction. Interest in certain skills, certain subjects or activities, when warmly encouraged and permitted to grow undisturbed, will advance stage after stage. These early supported periods in any developing child can lay a foundation for future accomplishments. But, as Jean Cocteau, one of the most creative artists of the 20th century, said, "An artist does not skip steps. If he does, it is a waste of time, because he has to climb them later." There is always a gradual progression from the simple to the complex before a skill becomes spontaneous.

A complete focus on and an unceasing engrossment in a special sphere or subject is the key to success when aspiring after knowledge and skills, and the fulfillment of higher achievement. In every case of exceptional achievement you will find the person was isolated with their work by circumstance, condition, or choice with complete concentration on that particular activity to the exclusion of almost everything else.

Even consider the case of an idiot savant. Someone rated deficient in ordinary mental powers, who delivers amazing answers to complex questions some would not attempt to answer. Here again we must accept that an information resource had to be conveniently present. Not one iota of knowledge or information can be generated out of a void. There must be someone's hand of guidance providing the learning opportunity and coaching.

I had an experience in my own life that demonstrates how uninterrupted concentration and coaching can produce surprising skills. When I was about nine years old, my parents had an accomplished pianist rooming and boarding in our home. For whatever reason, probably I had shown an interest in the piano in our living room, our tenant helped me pick out keys corresponding to notes on a piano score on the music stand. She showed me how to place my hands to reach the necessary keys and coaxed me to work at it, which I did.

I became fascinated with this exercise, working steadfastly at it throughout the summer vacation from school (I had no other amusement and nothing else to occupy myself at the time). As the summer passed, I had memorized, with the boarder's encouragement and praise the work she had placed before me. It was the prodigious Beethoven's 'Sonata Pathetique.' The only piece in my repertoire; but, I'm told, I handled it with a certain degree of skill for my age.

Later on, in my mid-twenties, I decided that the piano might be a good diversion and might enhance my savoir-vivre. I enrolled at the MacPhail Center for the Arts. At my first weekly evening session I was asked, "Have you ever played the piano before?" My answer was yes, and I was asked to play something. I launched into Beethoven's 'Sonata Pathetique,' and continued until the teacher begged me to pause.

I was given some exercises, and was asked to return the following week with an assigned piece to perform. I kept this up for three weeks, working every available moment until the next session, memorizing that this finger goes there and that finger goes here, disinclined to explain my problem to the teacher. I quit the class abruptly without giving any reason, never having learned the fundamentals of reading music and playing the piano, I was embarrassed. Today, under certain circumstances socially, I have performed my one number, amazing my audience, but declining modestly if asked to play more. Shades of the widely featured Australian piano prodigy, David Helfgott.

When someone has a consuming curiosity about a certain activity, subject or field of interest, the only limitations to becoming practiced and skillful and well-versed in that chosen interest is the availability of the information or coaching they seek, physical ableness or disability (but not entirely), and the intensity of their hunger to gain the knowledge and skills. Sir Isaac Newton, the English physicist and mathematician who conceived the idea of universal gravitation after seeing an apple fall from the tree in his garden, was asked how he had discovered this premise. He answered, "By thinking of it continually." Complete focus and unceasing engrossment in a particular sphere is the key to higher achievement.

The electrifying Russian piano virtuoso, Vladimir Horowitz, grew up in a musical environment, and spent his entire life from birth with a ferocious discipline in music to the exclusion of everything else. Just as many other famous musicians, including Bach, Mozart, Beethoven, Rachmaninoff, Schubert, Chopin, Liszt, Mendelssohn, Saint-Saens, and Brahms. He listened to music almost from the time of his birth. His mother was a pianist and teacher trained at the Royal Music School in Kiev, Russia. She practiced piano constantly at home; and, when she wasn't practicing, she was teaching her children. The parents enrolled Vladimir before he was nine years old in the Kiev Conservatory that had trained many famous pianists, including Paderewski. There was an excellent climate for a music hopeful in a society that valued excellence, and was able to both foster talent and measure it.

Tracy Austin, the youngest U.S. Open tennis singles champion in history at the time and the youngest competitor at Wimbledon at fourteen years of age, came from a family devoted to the game. Her mother with Vic Braden, a close friend of the family and a noted tennis coach, won a doubles tennis tournament in Southern California while she was pregnant with Tracy. It was said that Braden had rolled tennis balls to Tracy in her crib and became her first mentor. Her mother enrolled her in a tennis program at a famous club when Tracy was two, barely big enough to hold a racket.

Judy Garland, known first for her casting in the role of 'Dorothy' in the 'Wizard of Oz' and one of the greatest of all entertainers, was born within a family of performers. She had said that from the time she could first remember there was music all of the time all over their house. As Frances Gumm she joined her two sisters in theatrical performances, debuting professionally when she was only two years old. Her actor father had taken over the New Grand Theater in Grand Rapids, Minnesota, where he and Judy's mother became a duo act. Her mother, because of her efforts to find success for her daughters, was seen as an obsessive stage mother. Judy later said she had been forced into her career by her parents.

The lives of luminaries in music, literature, art, theater, or sports always record many hours of labor and dedication to their careers before their achievements were gained. Many were driven to their goals from the time of their birth by someone and for whatever reason, and many found their motivation later in life. It was because of some kind of stimulus or a provocation that directed them to great heights in construction of their skills or knowledge in their field. And, of course, it is never too late for someone at any point in their life to realize a success or fulfill a dream.

When a display of special skill or inventiveness is recognized, it is commonly accepted that the person was born gifted. The words 'genius,' 'wisdom,' 'astute,' 'insight,' 'imagination,' 'prodigy,' and 'savant' all suggest someone with special capabilities, knowledge, or skill present in one's consciousness or lodged in one's memory at birth. This implies that it is not natural for any ordinary person to have such a talent. But, many ordinary people become extraordinary achievers with no fragment of intelligence or skill that could have been a 'gift' at birth from their forebears.

The degree of a spirited and prolonged pursuit of some type of skill or knowledge in a particular sphere of interest decides if 'you know your stuff,' 'have a good head for,' 'have a skilled ear or eye for,' or have a talent that can be judged at some level of genius. Curiosity does seem to be a driving force so remarkably unequal in people. It marks the level of intelligence or creativity among individuals and must be nurtured early in life.

There are some things generally embraced such as the belief in 'inborn skills' or 'inborn traits' almost universally accepted and commonly taken for granted that are really suppositional positions. This conviction is held by many without challenge. It can give comfort in covering or excusing one's failure to reach fulfillment of personal expectations when no other explanation seems available.

There are many people primed in some special interest, trained for some achievement in the arts, entertainment, sports or whatever whose skills remain unheralded because of the lack of recognition, luck of the draw, or discouragement. Public preference honors some achievements and disregards others depending upon what is in or out during a particular period of time, season, or generation. The reigning culture of the moment will reward some performers and bypass those that sing a different song or dance a different dance. One's ultimate destination in life is not always determined by one's nature, but by their exposure to the scheme of things and the times and place they were born into.

Nevertheless an outstanding characteristic of human behavior is that it is flexible and adaptable. We can change situations and behavior to meet our desires or needs. We sometimes profit from the wisdom or folly of those who have lived before us. We move forward by gaining an awareness of and adapting to the world around us. My mother wrote this little poem for my inspiration:

> *Some reach for stars that shine too high,*
> *Some reach for stars that are right near by,*
> *Some change their stars from day to day,*
> *Some chase all stars that come their way.*
> *But he who keeps one star in sight,*
> *And steadily follows it day and night,*
> *Will learn what wisdom tries to teach,*
> *And sometime find that star in reach.*

RENOWNED PEOPLE HAVE RISEN IN
GRADUAL STAGES

Those move easiest who have learn'd to dance.
Alexander Pope

Charles Dickens spent his childhood in Victorian England in poverty and hardship. He was humiliated working in his youth as a drudge at a blacking factory, and spent most of his life trying to keep his father out of debtors' prison. He had very little education beyond what he learned on the streets. Later he studied shorthand, determined to become a journalist to follow his father's vocation. An avid reader, he read all of the material he could get his hands on during breaks in his labors.

The pains of poverty in Dicken's youth, the characters and humiliating situations he was subjected to provided him with a free attitude and humor. All of this appeared recognizably in his works. . .'Oliver Twist,' 'David Copperfield,' and the well-remembered 'A Christmas Carol.' He acquired a collection of experiences and jargon from his hard life to fill many novels.

Passing time and experience will change the ordinary into the extraordinary. But, there must be an impetus, some kind of personal stimulus, then an encouraging hand to guide and direct. Along with this some persuasive force that sets the goals and keeps them in sight. As well, there must be the learning opportunity, the accessibility of information and training. This is necessary to gain the skills and knowledge essential to pursue to its fruition any advantage gained from a favorable set of circumstances.

I have discovered as well that among the luminaries of the past and today there may often be some condition existing that has favored prolonged and constant attention to a work or study. There has been isolation possibly because of a situation in life, ill-health, or personal conflict of some kind.

Leonardo da Vinci, the Italian painter, sculptor, architect, and engineer, was known for his paintings the 'Mona Lisa' and

'The Last Supper.' He left copious, disorderly notebooks with research of great scope. . .anatomy, architecture, hydraulics, weaponry, human flight, and much more. He apprenticed for 10 years beginning at age fifteen in a workshop of a famous painter and sculptor of the period. In his long apprenticeship he became at ease with and captivated by the companionship of great artists, craftsmen, and engineers of his day who were his teachers and stimulus.

Igor Stravinsky, an American born and raised in Russia and said to be one of the greatest composers of the 20th Century, was the son of the leading bass singer of the St. Petersburg Imperial Opera Company. He was given piano lessons at nine years, but developed slowly. He studied law, but his interest in his father's music prevailed. Rimsky-Korsakov, the famous Russian composer with the St. Petersburg Conservatory of Music, was the father of a fellow student and friend of Igor. Probably noting Igor's intense interest in music, the father volunteered to become his mentor. Certainly a rare opportunity for Igor. He became famous eventually only when 'The Firebird,' his ballet he composed drawing upon his training in orchestration with Rimsky-Korsakov, was performed by a Russian Ballet company in Paris in 1910.

Ludwig van Beethoven, the German composer, was born within a family of musicians. His alcoholic father started his musical education and forced him into his lessons. . .even waking him from sleep for practice. Later he formed some valuable friendships in exclusive circles in Bonn which brought him the opportunity to study briefly with Mozart in Vienna, and later with Franz Joseph Haydn, the famous Austrian composer. This was unparalleled coaching for anyone as well as a musician like Beethoven.

Music was the main if not the only entertainment in Europe during the age of these musicians, and it offered many opportunities for some young, budding students to secure excellent training by accomplished virtuosi. It would also be the spur for their heated interest in music, and the centers in Milan, Venice, and Vienna offered many opportunities for public audiences for student musicians.

Michelangelo, the sculptor, painter, and architect who decorated the Sistine Chapel and was sculptor of the famous 'Pieta,' said that he had "sucked in the hammer and chisels I used for my statues from my mother's milk." He had been nursed by the wife and daughter of stone carvers. He gained his skills making copies of works by master painters, as did most all of the great artists. Born into a family of high position and wealth, and, because of an interest in drawing, he was permitted to enter a painters' workshop in Caprese at age fourteen. Later he entered a special atelier in the Medici Gardens. This was a special opportunity. It was the pattern of the day for budding artisans, if fortunate, to be placed as an apprentice in an atelier or artist's workshop under the tutelage of an accomplished virtuoso taking assignments to assist in the production of the virtuoso's commissioned works.

John Singer Sargent, one of the revered impressionist painters, was described as an American born in Italy, studied in France, painted like a Spaniard, looked like a German, and spoke like an Englishman. His mother, who was quite an amateur artist herself, was the daughter of a wealthy merchant. John was raised in Italy. His mother took him around to all the fine museums, and provided him with a nice education in the arts. He studied classical drawing in Paris at the Academy of Fine Arts. He became known for his many fine portraits including 'Madame X,' the painting of Madame Gautreau that caused a scandal at the Paris Salon.

Johann Sebastian Bach was born into a family of musicians and composers. . .generations of trained organists and town musicians. Early on he saw himself as an heir of the craft's tradition. He was orphaned at ten and lived with his oldest brother, a pupil of a famous organist and composer. His brother gave him his first training. Wed to the organ from early in his life, he was appointed a church organist at age eighteen.

Giuseppe Verdi, the Italian composer of 'La Traviata,' 'Rigoletto,' and the 'Ave Maria,' came from Parma and was the son of an illiterate innkeeper of low station. His first interest in music came when he heard the sound of the organ in the church in his village. Encouraged by his father, he received his first music lessons from an organist in their village. Later he was befriended by a brewer for whom he worked as an assistant in the small town of Busseto. The brewer was also President of the Philharmonic Society. The brewer provided money so that Giuseppe could go to Milan and try for entrance into the Conservatory.

However, Giuseppe was rejected at the Conservatory as lacking in musical talent, so he began the study of musical composition on his own. Later a musician at the Teatro alla Scala opera house agreed to take him on as a pupil. With this training he composed some operas and other works without success; and, experiencing a tragedy in his family at that time, decided to give up his musical career.

After a period at other activities, the manager of La Scalla pressed him to renew his work as a composer. With this prodding, among other works, Giuseppe produced the opera 'Nebuchadnezzar.' This opera was performed at the La Scalla with overwhelming success. He finally became famous over all of Italy because of this opera.

Long periods of labor, struggle, or failure, are common patterns that repeat themselves in the lives of those who have gained fame. As Georges-Louis Buffon, the French naturalist, said, "Genius is nothing but a greater aptitude for patience."

Leopold Mozart, the father of Wolfgang Amadeus, accurately remarked that there was no better place for a musical prodigy to be born than in Salzburg, Austria, a major music center. The father was a competent violinist and the author of a famous treatise on violin playing. He dedicated himself to the cultivation of musical skill in Wolfgang Amadeus. His domineering manner painfully inhibited his son's personality, but nurtured his musical skill and forced a sense of mission. The father pushed his career with a ceaseless round of touring. Wolfgang, first presented to a public audience at age six, was on tour more than half the time until he was fifteen. The touring, so early in life, did permit him to experience a broad range of music and musicians. . .music composed in that age and performed across Europe.

Franz Joseph Haydn, Austrian composer who was called the

father of the symphony, got a start on his career when he impressed the choirmaster of the Cathedral of St. Stephen in Vienna. The choirmaster was touring the countryside looking for choristers, and admired the quality of Haydn's eight-year-old voice. Franz was invited to the choir school of St. Stephen, and there he acquired a wide range of musical training and experience.

By the time his voice changed he was teaching aristocratic youths music, and was providing music for dances and serenades. Later he gained the interest of a grand patron, Prince Paul Anton, who owned a large celebrated orchestra. Prince Anton hired him to conduct his orchestra, furthering and supporting Franz's career.

Edward Gibbon, author of the classical work 'The Decline and Fall of the Roman Empire,' was an English historian and a member of England's House of Commons. He had been born into a family of rank and wealth. He was sickly as a child, and in his isolation was drawn into reading books. He had read all of the books on English history that were available by his fifteenth birthday. He was cared for by an aunt following his mother's death when he was only nine.

The aunt nurtured his interest in reading and history. He had said that continuous random reading was the comfort of his lonely hours.

Pablo Ruiz Picasso was born in Malaga on the southern coast of Spain in 1881. His father taught drawing and painting at a school of arts and crafts, and was said to be an unsuccessful painter of pigeons and household pets. Pablo's biographers have been confused because of his tendency to fable-spinning, but it is apparent Picasso received his necessary beginner training and stimulation from his father. When the family moved to Barcelona he entered a School of Fine Arts at which his father had taken a teaching post.

Pablo experimented widely during these early years, changing direction and style again and again apparently trying to escape his father's influence. At age sixteen, he entered the prestigious Royal Academy of San Fernando in Madrid, but stayed less than a year rebelling against its traditionalist teachings. However, over these periods he received all of the basics of drawing mechanics and the traditional methods of training typical for skilled artists of that day.

At this time Pablo developed scarlet fever, and spent a period in recuperation, maturing and becoming more independent from his family. He made a real effort to improve his drawing mechanics, and joined a group of young artists in Barcelona who introduced him to the style of painting that rejected naturalism with the use of evocative and symbolic imagery and color. However, his rebellious nature was always reflected in a wide diversity of styles from the natural to the bizarre.

Herman Melville, author of the great American epic 'Moby Dick,' was thought by his father to be mentally slow and backward. Herman was still a youth when his family fell into poverty. He tried clerking in a bank, selling in a store, and unsuccessfully teaching. Finally, he signed on as a cabin boy on a merchant ship from New York to Liverpool, England, at the age of twenty. Then, continuing his experience at sea, he signed on to a whaling boat to the South Seas, and suffered three brutal years on whalers.

Melville's experiences included the brutality of life on the ships, floggings, desertion, escape to an island, and living with friendly natives who turned out to be cannibals. He was part of a mutiny in Tahiti that ended with a stretch on the frigate United States. Why or how he became a writer, of course, is not known. But, his wild and rugged experiences in his years at sea could have filled many books.

Many works of famous composers in the past have not been familiar to the general public, and a few of their compositions have lived on only because of their acceptance and popularity. Common to many of the early musicians, they were born into families with strong musical influence. Their training on musical instruments and composition usually began early in life.

Such was the background of Sergei Prokofiev, known best by the public for the classic 'Peter and the Wolf.' This has been a lesson for children on the instruments in an orchestra. Probably as well, his ballet 'Romeo and Juliet.' He was introduced to the piano as an infant by his mother. She urged him at age five to make up little pieces. At age thirteen, she entered him into the St. Petersburg Conservatory of Music in Russia, where so many great musicians were trained. There he studied with Rimsky-Korsakov and other famous musicians of the day. Legends that portrayed these musicians as rare prodigies overlook the convenience of superior training and education.

Leaping forward to the advent of jazz, among legendary figures were George Gershwin, the popular American composer, and his brother, Ira, who wrote his lyrics. George had been given piano lessons in childhood. He was raised in Manhatten, New York's lower east side neighborhood that also molded Irving Berlin, whom George idolized. George Gershwin, early in his life, became rapt in the casual freedom of Tin Pan Alley. This was a district on 28th Street from 6th Avenue to Broadway in New York near his home. It took its name from sounds of the pianos in the studios of sheet music publishers up and down the street. It was likened to people banging on tin pans.

George developed a piano style from the player piano and from black musicians he watched and heard in Harlem. He began his career by plugging the songs of songwriters to the publishers up the street before writing on his own. George Gershwin scored his first success with the song 'Swanee' that was popularized by Al Jolson, the 'jazz singer' and movie star.

Caught up in the frenzy of show business, he wrote musical upon musical. His interest in show business and his music consumed his whole life to the exclusion of everything else. This has been typical, of course, of overachievers. But what would he have become if he had been born and lived in Des Moines, Iowa? What if he did not have such a musical environment and learning opportunity? George died suddenly and prematurely of a brain tumor at the age of thirty-nine..

Tennessee Williams, the Pulitzer Prize winner for his play 'Streetcar Named Desire,' was the author who introduced to theater such previously taboo subjects as homosexuality, nymphomania, castration, and cannibalism. He once wrote, "A morbid shyness once prevented me from having much direct communication with people, and possibly that is why I began to write." Most of his works came from the stresses of his early family life, and from his homosexuality. His dramas reeked of the unhappiness, loneliness, and the sexual anxiety of his life.

Certainly, in the matter of physical sports, the difference in body, arms, and legs, the variation in the size, shape, and density of bones and flesh are determined to the greatest degree by genetic coding and passed along at birth from the lineage of the parents. But again, the persuasive force must be present; and, sum and substance of great sports figures, there is always perseverance and patience, and intensive, prolonged training and experience.

Arnold 'Arnie's Army' Palmer was the son of Milfred J. 'Deacon' Palmer, a golf professional and grounds worker. Arnie began playing golf at four years of age with a set of clubs his father had cut down to his size. And, of course, was trained and spurred on by his father's interest and concern.

Bjorn Borg gained a place as the world's number one tennis player winning the Wimbledon again and again. His father, a master table tennis player, won a city table tennis championship in their hometown of Sodertalje, Sweden, near Stockholm. The father's prize was a tennis racquet. He gave his son Bjorn the prize. At the age of nine, this was Bjorn's first tennis racquet. Bjorn immediately became dedicated to the sport devoting every free hour. By chance he met Percy Rosberg in Sodertalje, the best tennis coach in Sweden, who was in town scouting players. Bjorn began his training with Rosberg at age ten. He practiced and trained seven days a week at the Salk Club in Stockholm.

Martina Navratilova began her tennis career under the tutelage of her father, a Czech tennis great. Both of her parents were skilled tennis players. Her grandmother, Agnes Semanska, ranked among the leading Czech women's tennis players. Martina also benefited and was spurred to success by sponsorship by the Communist government. No doubt where her persuasive force and training came from.

John Patrick McEnroe, Jr. began his tennis career as well under the tutelage of his father who continued to manage his career and that of his brother. Always an early learning opportunity and someone or something to spur it along.

Jimmy Connors' mother also was a professional tennis instructor. Not in the genes, but a willing professional trainer, and someone to set goals, support, and encourage.

Michael Jeffery Jordan, the basketball star that played with the Chicago Bulls, was encouraged by his parents to become skilled in sports as an area in which blacks had gained success. His father put up a backyard basketball court at their home when Michael was thirteen. Rejected when he first tried out for high school basketball because he was too short, grew four inches before his junior year. He left high school with top honors in basketball at 6 feet 6 inches tall.

Billie Jean King won the Wimbledon singles six times and doubles ten times. She was born into an athletic family drilled in physical fitness with a father who was a baseball and basketball player. Her mother was a standout swimmer, and her brother was a major league baseball pitcher. Inclined to play football with the boys in her neighborhood, her father steered his daughter away from football and into tennis. She played this sport with a passion. Her physical attributes, her physical body makeup and strengths were probably inherited from her parents that gave her advantages in power and endurance. But, her skills came from her opportunity to be involved in sports and the opportunities to learn physical skills from her athletic family.

Glen Cunningham, the 'Kansas Ironman' track and field star, is an example of someone gaining fame through adverse circumstances. Glen was burned badly in a schoolhouse fire that killed his brother. A long, slow, determined recovery and strength building by running to heal his badly burned limbs, was the stubborn discipline that spurred him to star as a mile runner and set a world record as a track athlete. What greater inducement and propulsion could there be?

Alfred 'Al' Unser, Sr. and Robert William 'Bobby' Unser grew up in the sport of race driving. They were the sons of a race driver and garage owner. Their environment and associations were completely with auto racing and racing drivers. Both Bobby and Al were Memorial Day Classic 'Indy

'500' winners supported by a racing family of three brothers and two uncles. A tradition of steering their way to racing car achievements. Al won the Indy in 1970, 1971, 1978, and 1987. Bobby won it in 1968, 1975, and l981.

Paul Robeson, All-American football star at Rutgers and famous black baritone singer and actor, is an example of someone whose inherited *physical characteristics* shaped his life and his career. His father, the Reverend Robeson, was a big man with a beautiful, resounding speaking voice. Paul's uncles also were big, powerful men. His size led him to excel in football and other athletics in high school. Blessed with the deep, rich voice inherited from his father and uncles, he sang in the glee club in high school, and was asked to star in Shakespeare's 'Othello' by the drama club...as the only student in the school to fit the role of a large black man.

Robeson worked hard in high school, and gained a four-year scholarship to Rutgers through a scholastic competition. . .a school noted for great football teams. He was isolated from other students because of his race, and dogged by prejudice throughout his career. At Rutgers, besides starring in athletics, he went into speaking and debate. With his booming voice, profiting by training received from his father, he was outstanding.

Paul Robeson later gained fame as the black giant in lead roles in 'Emperor Jones,' Symon the Cyrenian,' 'All God's Chillun Got Wings.' He had been coached and encouraged by Eugene O'Neill, the Pulitzer Prize and Nobel Prize winner for literature, to use his height and physique and his dark features to his advantage. He sang many concerts with his beautiful voice. . .mostly negro spirituals and folk songs from the South.

Margaret Mead, the renowned anthropologist, lived a life that surely was dominantly influenced by her parents' views of ethics and sex. They were agnostics. Her father scoffed at religious rites of any kind, was considered by some near him to be insensitive to other human beings, and was without humor. When the father strayed from the fold, these happenings were simply overlooked by the rest of the family.

Margaret really began her career at twenty-three, leaving her husband, an Episcopal minister, to go to the Samoan Islands alone to study the sexual habits of the natives. Her name became associated with sexuality and guilt-free love. Her works were said to have led to an era of permissiveness. Her provocative ideas caused many debates, and there were those who strongly disputed the truth of the findings expounded in her writings.

Margaret Munnerlyn Mitchell was born in November 1900 in Atlanta, Georgia. Here is an example of an early life with an environment and associations that led almost inevitably to her success as a novelist. Though the war between the States had ended at least 35 years before her birth, Georgians were still in their hearts a part of the Confederate States of America, honoring their Confederate dead and the battles they had fought. They continued to feel as a conquered people in a conquered territory. The attack and burning of Atlanta was relived over and over; and, wherever people gathered, the Civil War was fought anew.

Margaret Mitchell had listened over and over to the lurid details of the Civil War, and the life and characters in that era of life. There were endless graphic tales that her grandmother related as well as those told by veterans of the war and by the women left behind to fight their own kind of war.

She did study and become a writer at the Atlanta Journal, and had held a desire to become a published author. However, she had little if any confidence in her writing ability. Accident prone, she suffered several episodes of injury that required confinement, and finally one that would cause her death. One of these episodes kept her shut in for a prolonged period when she began to write the one and only work she would ever publish.

When a publisher's representative was visiting in Atlanta, she was prodded by friends to turn over to him a disorganized, incomplete manuscript. The editors of the publisher then helped Margaret organize and complete the book titled, 'Gone With The Wind.' The rest of the story you already know.

Emily Dickinson was considered the foremost woman poet from the United States. Starting with no special background, attending Amherst Academy in Massachusetts and Mount Holyoke Seminary, she began to withdraw more and more from the world about her. She was very shy and in poor health. She concentrated her time writing in her seclusion on love, death, and immortality. The only poems published during her lifetime were published against her wishes and anonymously. Her sister, Lavina, turned her poems over for publishing four years after Emily's death. Another example of someone in seclusion because of an unusual condition that drove all of her attention to bear on one activity and direction.

Louisa May Alcott wrote one of the best-loved stories in American literature, 'Little Women.' Her father, Amos Bronson Alcott, was a philosopher, writer, and excellent teacher. . .and educated his own children. The Ralph Waldo Emersons and Henry David Thoreau, great names in literature, were friends and neighbors in the Massachusetts community where she was raised. Her first writings came from experiences during long, lonely months trying to find work in Boston, and later nursing soldiers during the Civil War. Her great success came when a publisher in Boston suggested that she write a story for girls. She wrote about a family in the book. The family, of course, was the Alcott family, and the story related experiences in their lives.

An example of success incidental to a discovery during day to day labor was John Deere, the famous farm implement manufacturer. Quite a step from the literary world, he had received no more than a common school education in Vermont. His first work was as a blacksmith's apprentice at the age of seventeen. He did acquire the skills of a blacksmith with this training. Then observing some of the inefficiencies of the iron and wood plows he was repairing, he beat out of an old circular saw blade of hard-tempered steel the plate for a plow used to turn over the earth. It was a spectacular and historical success.

John Milton, noted English poet of the 1600s, known best for the blank verse epic 'Paradise Lost,' had a father steeped in learning and a composer of music. He said his father destined him early in childhood for the study of literature. He said that he developed "so keen an appetite that from my twelfth year scarcely ever did I leave my studies for bed before the hour of midnight." He spoke always as being grateful to his father for having inspired his vocation.

Auguste Rodin, born in Paris in 1840, became one of the most celebrated of the artists of his age. This most prolific sculptor's best known work is undoubtedly 'The Thinker,' so much copied, caricatured, and imitated today in so many ways. His father led a rather uneventful life as an office worker, and his mother was a devout woman from a farm family. Hardly the expected background or genetic source for a world-famous artist and artisan. Auguste attended a church school in Paris experiencing difficulty even learning to read and write. After a short unsuccessful period at the school, at age nine he was sent to an uncle who ran a boarding school, hopefully for a more intense training.

There, under severe discipline in poor surroundings, he became gentle and courteous with a shy, diffident voice that would follow him throughout his life. But, considered as a lost cause scholastically, at age thirteen the uncle sent him back to his family to begin his life virtually without an education. The father, frustrated, entered him into one of the free schools available in that day to be trained as an artisan. . .woodcarver, stone carver, goldsmith, jeweler or whatever that Auguste might hopefully acquire as a trade.

One day, noting other students at the trade school modeling in clay and making plaster casts, he decided this was something he might like to do. After completing this training at the free school, he tried three times to apply for entry into the distinguished Grande Ecole des Beaux-Arts in Paris, but was rejected each time. Then, to earn a living for himself, he drifted from porcelain factories, architectural plasterers and decorators, as well as assisting artisans, sculptors, and mold casters for all of the next 20 years. He worked at the most insipid tasks; but, as was his nature, without making any complaint. He lived in poverty as just one anonymous craftsman among many.

However, continuing to practice and study the arts, he was sharpening his skills. Then, after a long period of mediocrity, he was given an opportunity to join the studio of a successful sculptor. Here he was directed to produce models that were signed, as was the custom at that time, by the master sculptor as the master sculptor's own work.

Rodin finally gained his fame and commissions when he was thirty-seven when he entered, under his own name, a plaster cast at the Paris Salon. His figure, 'The Age of Bronze,' was so startlingly lifelike that other artists accused him of having taken the mold from a living model.

Ernest Hemingway, American novelist and short-story writer, was known as a craftsman whose terse style, with its dramatic understatement and superb dialogue, was to influence several generations of writers. He came from a conservative, well-heeled family in the plush, snobbish community of Oak Park, Illinois. His father, Dr. Clarence Edmonds Hemingway, was said to be the complete woodsman, hunter, marksman with rifle and shotgun, fisherman, and master of every technique for surviving in the wilderness. He was known as a real macho man's man. Ernest had the best of education both cultural and commercial that money could buy. He was afforded every kind of opportunity, tried everything, and his father's driving force demanded that he excel at whatever venture he attempted.

Hemingway was pursued throughout his life by an obsession to prove he was as tough and masculine and rugged as his father. But, on the flip side, his mother was said to have held a desire for twins, and often had dressed him and his sister alike in girl's dresses and hairstyles. As well, his sister, one and one-half years older, was always taller until puberty and able to best Ernest in running and other children's sports.

Probably because of this conflicting treatment in his early years, he thrust himself into dangerous and tumultuous situations around the world to the point of self-destruction. He exaggerated tales he related about these experiences, but had accumulated enough knowledge and encounters and hardening to fill many books . . .almost always writing about himself.

His desire to become an author was first fulfilled when he was twenty-four. He committed suicide at age sixty-two as his father had done when Ernest was only twenty-nine. He was forever overshadowed by his father's supermasculine image.

Harold (Hal) Prince, rightly nicknamed 'The Prince of

Broadway,' directed a wealth of the greatest Broadway musicals. He was raised in New York near the theater district. When only a child he was regularly taken by his parents to see theater productions; and, as early as age eight, began spending most of his time and interest with theater. This undoubtedly led to his successful career in theater as an adult. He directed, sometimes produced, many top-rated musicals that included 'Showboat,' 'Evita,' 'The Phantom,' and many more. He is still going strong. Here, as in every instance of a successful career, was the learning opportunity and the influence of his closeness to the theatrical life. Again, what would he have done had he been born and raised, not nearby the theater district of New York, but in a rural community such as Lindstrom, Minnesota.

Many great achievers have attempted to cover their skills and inventive methods in a shroud of mystery. Whether this was because of modesty or a desire to set themselves apart from the masses, they often seemed to nourish the inference that their outpourings of creativity may have been aroused by something out of the ordinary course of nature. There was and is a tendency to present themselves as visionaries with the source of their works obscured.

An example is this quote from a diary of Henry Wadsworth Longfellow, "I wrote last evening a notice of Allston's poems. After which I sat till twelve o'clock by my fire smoking, when suddenly it came to my mind to write the 'Ballad of the Schooner Hesperus,' which I accordingly did. Then I went to bed, but could not sleep. New thoughts were running in my mind, and I got up to add them to the ballad. I feel pleased with the ballad. It hardly cost me any effort. It did not come to me by lines but by stanzas."

Longfellow, an American poet, excellent linguist and translator of Dante's 'Divine Comedy,' and a professor at Bowdoin College in Maine, was born in 1807. His father was a Harvard graduate and a prosperous lawyer. His mother, a lover of music and literature, was descended from John Alden and Priscilla Mullen, a family legend which Henry described in his writing the 'Courtship of Miles Standish.'

Henry was sent to Bowdoin College when only fourteen (his

father was a trustee of that college), and then to Europe at age eighteen to prepare for a professorship in languages and literature. His poetry was never profound or powerfully original. The ballad 'The Wreck of the Hesperus' was prompted by a newspaper account of an actual wreck at sea at that time.

Undoubtedly such popular pieces on the surface appear to have been produced very quickly, without effort. However, the material for such works would have been gathered carefully into the mind over time. The experiences, knowledge, or information related to a particular composition, work of art, or other exceptional product, along with its impetus, must be accumulated and then imbued with the spirit to produce it.

Longfellow's explanation of working with a spontaneous burst of 'genius' as well as similar declarations by many other creative people leads to a super-abundance of suppositions and misinformation about the processes of the mind . . .and the 'born with' conviction.

There are many, many examples such as this one of Longfellow's in the lives of famous achievers and performers. But, they each show a persuasive force coming from somewhere, special learning opportunities, and a set of circumstances permitting constant attention to a certain area of activity or thought that resulted in the extraordinary or popular achievement. This is a pattern that will be found in every great accomplishment in art, musical performance and composition, writing, sports or in business. Not inherent differences in intelligence or skills, but differences in the driving influences and opportunities.

There is a position often held, related to the misconceptions about the source of great products of creativity and intelligence, that 'freshness' or creative vitality fades with age and is strong only in one's youth. This is a faulted belief or conclusion because only the reverse has been proven to be true. A professor of psychology at the University of California notwithstanding concluded from his study of the biographies of selected noted, creative people of the early 1900s and before, that the most productive range of creative careers falls between the ages of twenty-eight and forty-five. However, he must have overlooked or slighted the life expectancy tables that as late as 1920 were showing age fifty-four as the official average of life expectancy. And, much lower than that in the 1800s. Many of the creative greats of the long past died before reaching their forties.

There were great achievers, of course, that lived much longer. Johann Wolfgang von Goethe, the celebrated German sage and poet, said at his eighty-second year, "I am delighted to find that even at my great age ideas come to me the pursuit and development of which would require another lifetime." The truth is that the breadth and richness of a life and mind steeped in years of sensory and intellectual experiences and imagery provide a very rich well to draw upon. The mature mind overflowing with experience can dip successfully from this well for many choices to combine its memories into new forms and new directions.

Goethe was born in 1749 at Frankfurtam-Main, Germany. His father was a wealthy judge, and his mother was the daughter of the ruling burgomaster (or mayor) of Frankfurt. Goethe's influential father personally supervised his early education in languages, history, and the sciences of the time. He was sent at age sixteen to study law; and, after a brief hiatus because of ill health, received his degree and began practicing law with his father's help and guidance.

But, through his contacts he became more interested in the theater, literature, and the fine arts. His curiosity brought him great versatility as a poet, dramatist, novelist, and natural scientist.

George Bernard Shaw, the Irish dramatist, critic, and social reformer, after unsuccessful attempts, for the first time had a collection of his plays published at the age of forty-two. But his finest, 'Pygmalion' (which later became the musical comedy 'My Fair Lady'), and 'Androcles and the Lion' were published after he reached fifty-six. He continued to be productive, receiving the Nobel Prize in Literature at age sixty-nine. He was at work on a comedy at the time he died at age ninety-four.

Shaw was born in Dublin, Ireland, in 1856. He learned music from his mother, who gave lessons to support their family. He left schooling in Dublin to earn a living at age fifteen. At age twenty went to London, and, while struggling unsuccessfully as a general writer, read everything he could find and attended the meetings of musical, literary, and political groups. At thirty-two he became a music critic for the London Star and later The World. He became known as one of the leading music and drama critics in London working for the Saturday Review before writing the popular and well-known 'Candida' in 1898.

Igor Stravinsky composed many of his major works during his seventies and eighties. And, of course, Anna Mary Robertson (Grandma Moses), a farmer's wife who began painting in her seventies, gained fame for her primitive works documenting rural life.

There are many, many examples of creative achievement late in life. As were Thomas Alva Edison, Victor Hugo, Claude Monet, and Titian who produced some of their best work in their seventies and eighties. Pablo Picasso, the painter, and Arthur Rubinstein, the pianist, were still at work in their nineties. Arthur Fiedler, the conductor, was actively working until a short while before his death at age eighty-eight. And, Giuseppe Verdi composed 'Falstaff' when he was eighty years young.

All of these famous personages drew their skills and knowledge from lives filled to the brim with curiosity, constant activity, and a wealth of fruitful experiences. Only minds well-stocked with rich experiences and memories are those capable of producing products of earthshaking innovation and cultural breaktroughs. Marcus Tullius Cicero, the Roman orator and writer, said, "Give me a young man in whom there is something of the old, and an old man with something of the young; guided so, a man may grow old in body, but never in mind."

Brilliant music, great performances or beautiful works of art must come from those who have learned their skills and gained their knowledge over time. They were never born to it. Their works were never created because of an especial condition in their genes or because of some special 'gift' passed on at birth. The skills and knowledge that gave cause for their achievements had to be acquired through a prolonged interest or practice spurred by some kind of driven impulse. The lives of all who have created something proclaimed by the masses as unique and special have always revealed some persuasive force, special learning opportunities, and unrelenting attention to their field or endeavor. A pattern of personal development that has so often led to great minds and unparalleled performances.

EACH WILL CHOOSE THEIR LIFE'S PATH

For man is man and master of his fate.
Alfred, Lord Tennyson

Genetic researchers at the top level in the advanced study of human genes have asserted in agreement that there is absolutely no scientific basis for any claim linking genetics to human behavior or intelligence. Their studies have shown that we are 97 percent genetically identical throughout the world's human population, and the differences in behavior or intelligence that vary from person to person have nothing to do with genetics.

There is something very wonderful about human intelligence and behavior, and the mind's and the body's processes. Something before which we all quite rightly must stand in awe. When seeing its work in writings of all kinds, and in many forms of the arts, experiencing its creations in music, dance, and the theater, it is often expressed as 'genius.' When observing a unique performance or improvisation, it is sometimes looked upon as something impersonal and removed from our own lives, a 'gift' that was given to a person at birth. But, there is no evidence of any kind that such a thing could be true.

How people behave, what they become or achieve, whether they embrace or are indifferent to accepted conduct or moral standards has more to do with reciprocal relationships and cultural orientations than genetic gifts from progenitors.

Behavior is an established disposition of the mind or character that is accustomed by frequent exposure to, often chosen, patterns of individual or group practice. In a disciplined home environment a person will tend to adhere to its cultural and moral direction. If left up to themselves for development or when guidance is limited, people are apt to accept readily any strong pattern in behavior or manner of living that may pass by. Moral conviction and special aspirations must be driven by concerned caregivers or other intimates.

There are certain men and women, such as those whose lives were touched upon in the preceding chapter, who have been especially honored and gained fame since the beginning of time. For whatever reason and in whatever field of activity, chosen individuals and their works have been heralded and chronicled in history as unipersonal and labeled as 'genius.' There could have been others, of course, in the same periods who may have deserved great praise for their works, but were not persons anyone bothered to hold commendable or memorialize. It is possible they were not at the right place at the right time, with the right works, or the right song.

The precise nature of special intelligence or inventiveness and the genesis of celebrated accomplishments may never be completely explained. But, there is nothing in body or mind preexistent about this, nor such a thing causing any socially threatening or unacceptable behavior.

Attempts have been made to understand the celebrated achievers through the study of their art, their music, or their writings. Their products have been brought together for comparison, and terminology has been coined for their discussion. Intellectual brilliance and innovation and the notion of 'giftedness' have posed riddles that psychologists and educators have tried to answer without success. Endless studies have been recorded and theories expounded, but always fruitlessly. Conflicting theories have been proposed by each of the branches of knowledge and scientific authority.

After all of the proposed answers, science now explains simply, that intelligence and creativity are variables, not directly observable, something that a person can possess and varies among people. The only agreed position of the scientists today is that intelligence or the source of hailed accomplishments, as well as that of dissolute behavior, is something that exists in all of us.

There are two natural conditions that separate the human animal from all other living creatures upon the earth. Freedom of will (as it has been said since that time in the Garden of Eden), and the faculty to form new thoughts and ideas from existing information. These human peculiarities have given us the capacity for each to choose their own course in life and their destiny.

When we enter this world at birth we come into it with a mind not yet affected or directed by any experience other than in utero. Each child is an individual creation that is unfolding. A newborn will bring with it an instinctive physical desire for food or liquid, for warmth or protection. Even before birth the fetus can learn something about the world it will enter. Whatever a baby can sense or hear in the womb will affect its developing mind. It will recognize its mother's voice. It may have some apprehension for pain or danger. There are fears learned from the sounds heard while encased in the womb or emotions passed along by the mother. When at last it is born, it has a disposition to recognize what is good for it and what may harm it.

Normally we bring with us the dexterous fingers, hands, and limbs that are natural for the human animal. We have vocal powers, when trained, that permit us to communicate with one another. As well, we are programmed to make more of our own kind, but there is no knowledge or selective behavior actually present in our consciousness or entrusted within our memory at our birth. *And, the mind, before experiencing anything in this world, must be considered void of any knowledge or ideas.* Our ultimate destination in life is not commanded by each one's nature but by our exposure to the scheme of things, the place we are born into, those we encounter, and the experiences we face in life.

As John Locke, the English physician and philosopher, said in his writing 'An Essay Concerning Human Understanding,' "When life begins, the mind, before it receives the impressions gained by experience, is a blank slate. . .tabula rasa." However, human infants are born ready to take on the world. Many things are happening in their minds. Memory is very much developed, and they are recording carefully each new experience. . .each new sound. . .each new sensation . . .all of the events going on about them. They sift through a jumble of voice sounds from family members and others, hopeful of grasping some meaning or direction. . .quite able to learn from the time of their birth.

In that first onslaught of experiences they learn to recognize those critical to their care and feeding, as well as what makes them comfortable and what makes them uncomfortable. They are experiencing, remembering, and questioning as soon as they enter the world. Then when the seed of curiosity is planted in some way, and the beginnings of experience and learning is rooted in place, insight springs forth. It puts out its branches and leaves, and blossoms into being. There is a law that nature be continuous.

This ongoing activity of experiencing, remembering, and questioning goes on throughout life's onward course. Accumulating and assembling, considering all information, sensations, impacts, and reactions consciously and subconsciously.

We are each born with certain physical peculiarities; and, as in a spray of roses, no two are completely identical. As the chromosomes gather and multiply in each new being, they spell out its personal physical composition. During the maturization of the reproductive cells, the genetic information is reshuffled in so many ways that each conceptus receives an entirely original physical composition. A composition which has never occurred before and will never happen again. Like a fingerprint, each is unique and irreplaceable. These physical differences in development, of course, explain how some individuals can be born with winning, overpowering, and attracting physical and biomechanical advantages.

Nature has a capricious manner of giving each person attributes that differ by degrees from raving beauty, run-of-the-mill plainness, or just ill-fated ugliness in features, bone and body. This is carried out with a hit or miss attitude, fulfilling some persons and constraining others. The same is true of muscle prowess, shape and size randomly engendered with dissimilarities either specifically suited to certain physical or sports activities, or sufficing only to carry one about in a limited way in day to day activities.

Also physically, a quality of voice sounds can be an advantage for some from birth which eventually gives them stentorian tones that can thunder throughout a concert hall, or others gain bell-like voices that please, or some with simply pipes that grate or shriek or whisper.

Without a doubt these physical singularities will have an

inviolable effect upon fortunes and insufficiencies as well as upon behavior. It is said that life's lovelies most often breathe the air of success while homely people gain only societal and workplace prejudice. Tall men most often do better than short men, and overweight people have to fight against discrimination.

The advantages and handicaps of appearance are commonplace. The television program 20/20 on the ABC network twice aired tests they had made that showed how pretty women or good-looking men were given hiring preferences over plain people with equal qualifications. Tests also showed that trial juries could be influenced in their judgments by good-looking people in cases presented in court. Appearance handicaps, of course, often can be enhanced or improved with training or therapy or cosmetics as many physical peculiarities can be. Or, they may be abused depending upon practices or misuse just as the mastery of learning sometimes can be encouraged or neglected.

It is evident that physical blessings or disadvantages should be recognized as early as one can in life. Then polished or corrected for improvement to whatever degree may be possible or called for. And, then exploited.

In a discussion of the progression in the development of exceptional people or those with immoderate behavior in adults or children, we need not speculate about where intelligence and creativity originate. Many psychologists and educators have, and they have searched uncertainly for an explanation of how the brain and its neurons work masterminding a host of incredibly complex processes to produce our thinking, walking, feeling, and talking. . .as have many neuroscientists. *All of their conclusions and theories have been inconclusive anyway.*

In this study we will not be concerned with any definition of intelligent or successful people, or providing a general model of the brilliant or creative personality, nor type the criminal or amoral temperament . All attempts to list and bracket the personal characteristics that have favored artists, writers, composers, intelligentsia, and others who have been immortalized throughout history have failed. Whether their personal lives were played as neurotics, criminals, scholars, or fools does not explain their works, deeds, or particularity, or predict their capabilities.

There is a progressive path that has led famous people of the past and today to their success, just as there is a degenerative path that has led many to immoral, criminal, of antisocial behavior. Intelligence, inventiveness, and moral conduct are the birthright of the human race, but they must be acquired progressively in stages throughout each individual's experiences in life.

There is a direct correlation between intelligence and experience. Anyone who would aspire to become outstanding as an artist, writer, scientist, astronaut, doctor, lawyer, tennis or basketball star, or achieve excellence in any field must pay the price. He or she must follow link by link a progressive chain of training and experience, omitting not one link in order to gain perfection. Every great achiever has had a developmental history growing from childhood trial performances to adult primacy. Never has there been a case of excellence at birth in any field. George Gershwin did not leap from the womb asking for a piano.

There are some who may feel incorrectly that they were shortchanged at birth . . .that they should have been born with some ability standing above that of all others. A feeling that fate or heredity should have given them some unusual readiness in inborn creative power, a singular intellect, artistic bent, deftness in a craft, competence in athletics, or a musical gift. When people fail in an attempt to play an instrument of some type. . .when they fail to gain success in some trial or test. . .they sometimes blame their forebears for not passing along some latent 'talent.' That special thing that some may say cuts the mustard, and separates the sheep from the goats.

On the other hand, there are some who may feel they have something special that they can't seem to explain. Something they do that comes so easy that they suspect it came from a spiritual force, if not some supernatural force. But, it may always be explained by a forceful, companionate influence somewhere in their background coupled with intense training or study that made their skill or knowledge spontaneous.

We have to accept that primordial creation. . .magic. . .is beyond human power, and certainly beyond the grasp of the human mind or body. Ability or skill cannot originate out of a vacuum. Of one thing we can be certain, skills or intelligence cannot be fetched out of a void. Information can never be produced 'ex nihilo' (from nothing).

There must be three things present in one's background before an extraordinary achievement, performance, human trait can burst forth: An appropriate learning opportunity or indoctrination; a persuasive force or influence of some kind; and a compulsive absorption of one's time and effort and interest in the chosen subject or activity.

There is clear evidence of the way the mind's well of information and experience is stockpiled, processed, and delivered into combinations that bring about our accomplishments. There are as well those human tendencies that spur or obstruct learning and originality of thought. There are those things that have been practiced by chance or deliberate purpose by many of the famous who have displayed some kind of special knowledge or proficiency.

President Teddy Roosevelt, a Nobel Peace Prize winner, wrote that the person who experiences success is not a genius but someone who has merely ordinary qualities and has developed those ordinary qualities to a more than ordinary degree.

FIXED MINDS AND FAULTED REASONING

The trouble with people is not that they don't know,
but that they know so much that ain't so.
                                        Josh Billings

Prejudice and conditioned thinking can rob people of their individuality, and the quality of being easily approached by others. And, the quality of being constantly conscious of the lives, habits, and emotions of others. This can become a part of a culture, it can cause deep rifts between societies, faiths, nationalities, and other bodies. When it becomes a part of the personal makeup or personality of an individual. . .looking inward instead of outward. . .it can become the cause of many of the mind games, personality clashes, corrupt and deviated behaviors that occur in the lives around us.

Misleading information in the news and other sources often instills in people faulted beliefs that they will cling to and be ready to 'go the bundle for' if they are ever challenged. They will defend hotly that which he or she has heard or read and perceived to be true. When faced with information in conflict with their position or perception, even when there is a true and logical explanation, they will hold to their view stubbornly.

Faulted perception can come from listening or reading and accepting without questioning a biased point of view offered by someone who has been given heed or admired. Sometimes a popular idea will take root from a political positioning. A proposition or supposition out of the news or from reports of science's studies may not be tested or questioned because the source appears to be reasonable enough and it supports a personal view. The nature of the information can become so important to a person that any message not consistent with that which has become a part of the person's mindset will be dismissed without any consideration of an opposite view.

Much of the information in the news reports today is formed of extrapolations by the media from announcements regarding observations in laboratories, genetic studies, and statistical data.

Usually commentaries by psychologists, social scientists, Ph.D.s, educators, or psychiatrists. . .individuals not certifiable as professional microbiologists or members of the Genome Project teams. The best chance is that a great part of the information we are asked to consume regarding health, behavior, and intellectual attainment is unverified conjecture rather than solid information rooted in clear evidence. We all know how quickly positioning on the dangers and effects of some foods or supplements or lifestyles are changed or reversed from one report to another.

An open mind will reflect upon every new experience and bit of information faced, and weigh its correctness and supporting evidence carefully. And, hear all propositions and all sides of theories. We should accept as fact only documented and proven information, and recognize hypothetical reports for what they are. . .often only conclusions or guesswork based upon uncertain evidence. Of course, it would be just as wrong to doubt everything as it would be to believe everything. Information that may challenge a broad-based body of knowledge that has received long time support should certainly be treated guardedly. But, well-worn modes of thinking, practices that follow timeworn customs, or have had long unquestioned acceptance should be reconsidered whenever there is new evidence or reassessment of their validity.

Most of us have forgotten much that we should have remembered, and remember much that we should have forgotten. The information we cleave to in our minds is sometimes distorted by our preconceived notions. When a position has been long adopted, it is a characteristic of human wont to gather everything to it that will agree or fortify that position. Then one will search and grasp any information that will bear our their belief. Any information that does not suit a closely held belief will be rejected or ignored. This is something that has been called 'confirmation bias.'

So often we will choose what we wish to believe. Positions and actions are usually self-generated and self-determined by personal principles, personal loyalties, and self-indulgence. 'Impartiality,' the 'open mind,' the 'unprejudiced observer' are most often simply figures of speech. We all have our prejudices and preferences.

Our reasonableness can be influenced by our personal wishes. New propositions are usually judged according to prevailing opinions. The 'herd instinct' will impel people to conform and resist new thinking that opposes generally accepted ideas. There is an overwhelming disinclination to abandon long, deep-felt points of view because of the comfort of the friendly social environment it provides. When exposed to something unfamiliar or new, or a rebuff of someone's position on a subject, most will attack or ridicule any alternative information offered.

It is difficult for most people to accept changes in their grasp of information. New wrinkles in accepted positions or understandings are not anticipated and not only cause some surprise at a contradiction, but are puzzling and confusing. Many great discoveries were thought to be absurd in light of prevailing wisdom.

When a new concept, philosophy or scheme of things is put forward, many may ignore it as being out of step with existing information. There are those who cannot open themselves to new perceptions lest they endanger the security of their established presumptions or convictions.

People generally perceive what they want to perceive and believe what they want to believe. How would most people view these statements?

Charles A. Lindbergh was the sixty-seventh person to cross the Atlantic Ocean in an airplane nonstop.

Noah Webster never published the 'Webster's Dictionary.'

The famous painter, James Whistler, is well-known because of his classic painting 'Arrangement in Gray and Black.'

Inaccurate, incomplete understanding, or inattention can

make these three statements appear incorrect. They are not. They are as true as can be. Charles Lindbergh was the first to make *a solo flight* across the Atlantic Ocean, but many had made the flight across before the famous flight of the 'Lone Eagle.' Noah Webster named his dictionary *'The American Dictionary.'* Many of the publishers have printed and marketed a Webster's Dictionary. . .by our laws the name 'Webster' could not be copyrighted or registered as a trademark. James Whistler's famous painting that he titled, *' Arrangement in Gray and Black,'* has been commonly referred to as 'Whistler's Mother.'

As Georg Lichtenberg, the German physicist and satirist, said, "The most dangerous untruths are truths moderately distorted." It is very human to hold views because of misconceptions that come from pride, slanted self-interest, and preconceived judgments. A person will not admit this even to himself. People do tend to perceive what they want to perceive, and determine what they wish to determine.

As an ideal, the mind should be a place where all information and points of view will be welcomed. Someone likened this to an Open House where the invited, the most interesting, and the gate-crashers were all received equally. We release the kaleidoscopic combinations of experiences and images stored in the library of our subconscious mind when we have unblocked the obstacles to open thought in our conscious mind.

The problem with the resistance to new ideas or information is that the new must so often displace strong beliefs already accepted and fixed in the mind...like the story about the psychiatrist's patient who insisted that he was dead. To change this strange belief, the psychiatrist asked him if dead men bleed. When the patient answered that they did not, the psychiatrist pricked the patient's finger and raised a drop of blood. When the patient saw this he said, "Well, I'll be damned. Dead men do bleed."

The unexpected awaits at every curve in the road throughout life. We benefit following a course that is open to all of the world's facts and information and not attached to commonly held beliefs or traditional thinking. And, to keep the mind always open to change. Niccolo Machiavelli, the Italian philosopher, wrote, "There is nothing more difficult to take in hand, more perilous to conduct, or more uncertain in its success, than to take the lead in the introduction of a new order of things."

IN ALL THE WORLD THERE IS NO ONE EXACTLY LIKE ME

There is no recipe of living that suits all cases. Each of us carries his own life-form. . .an indeterminable form which cannot be superseded by any other.

Carl Gustav Jung

We must realize what marvelous creatures we are! We are so wonderfully made. It is most important to hold an incorruptible respect for one's body and one's self in order to avoid the pitfalls of dishonesty and greed, inordinate sexual practices or a disregard for our laws and order of things. This is difficult with the mixed temporal messages from our media and entertainment providers.

The future can seem to be a narrow way through a craggy rock forest, torrential rivers, and bottomless ravines by both adults and youths unless they are prepared for it. In this complex world exploding with technology, there is something new to be learned every day. And, we are forced to keep up with its unslackening parade.

To live a sane and stable life, we need to recognize the wonderful form into which we have been created. There is a declaration of self-esteem, a remarkable credo of Virginia Satir, a therapist and teacher, that has said it so well, if I may quote briefly these excerpts from her book that she makes available:

"In all the world, there is no one else exactly like me. . .I own everything about me. . .my body, my feelings, my mouth, my voice, all my actions, whether they be to others or to myself. . .I own me. . .I am me, and I am OK!"

We take for granted the complex mental activities every person routinely performs day after day and hour after hour. Though unlike anything else that exists in the whole world, we are so accustomed to our automatic skills that we are apt not to realize how remarkable they are. A professor at Harvard estimated that the circuitry of the human brain could be sixty times the complexity of the entire United States telephone system. Yet we are so commonly unaware of those unseeable mental activities and processes so normal with all humans and so marvelous in their accomplishments.

Our minds have been likened to undiscovered gold mines. The brain that lies above our shoulders has an infinite capacity. Each of us see, hear, feel, taste, smell, and store in our minds barely five percent of what the human brain is capable of grasping and filing away. These are the images and data gathered from the day of birth. These are the scenes, the words, the sounds, everything that passes before each person throughout a lifetime. It has been said that, if the human brain could be taxed to work at only half of its capacity, you would be able to learn thirty languages, memorize an entire set of the Encyclopedia Britannica, and complete the courses of three dozen colleges.

Our minds store an incomprehensible immensity of learned data, visual images and sensory reactions, and auditory perceptions that we use in such unexplained and unexpected ways. Actually our minds hold several billion times more data than the fast computers we have today. Most of this information we can reach without hesitation or pause to search. It is a vast reference library without the need to leaf slowly through its pages. And, we can usually recognize immediately if certain information has not been stored there. Who was the mother of the mother of the first czar of Russia? No need for a search. You know immediately that it isn't up there.

The existence of mental processes that are active in the mind without conscious awareness was first studied scientifically by the French neurologist Jean-Martin Charcot in the 1800s through hypnosis. Sigmund Freud, a student of Charcot and considered the father of psychoanalysis, has been recognized as the first to map the unconscious world of the human mind. He compared the mind to an iceberg as having only one-eighth of it above the surface in the conscious and seven-eighths of it below the surface in the unconscious. He referred to the subconscious memory as a subterranean land of enormous size. Today it is the hope of neuroscientists everywhere to lift the veil on how the unconscious brain interacts with the conscious brain to influence cognition and behavior.

Within the last twenty-five years there has been greater sophistication of the psychological research, though many, many critical questions remain unanswered. Large steps have been made in the testing of neurological patients who have had accidental brain damage or undergone radical brain surgery. Scientists have discovered that the domain of the unconscious is far more limitless than even Freud had envisioned.

It is now believed that the brain's network has some 100 billion to 1 trillion nerve cells that coordinate thought and the senses as well as most all bodily activities. The mind could be made up of thousands of independent modules that are operating subconsciously performing different mental tasks and memory. . .constantly forging new connections and unraveling old ones responding to signals from the senses.

Qualified researchers have found that there can be vision without having a conscious awareness of seeing. Images sent so swiftly that they cannot be perceived by the conscious eye are still recognized and recorded by the subconscious mind. Information may be stored and then processed by the unconscious brain before ever reaching consciousness. And, there can be separation between conscious and unconscious thought. In other words, a person can be unaware of all the memories that live in the unconscious depths of the mind. These are the observations going unnoticed of what we have seen, heard or felt. The influence of the environment and associations going on about us. Subtle influences that could catch one off guard, and bear a powerful effect upon behavior for good or for bad. Instructing or divining our interests and curiosity and preferences.

Such research suggests that those subconscious modules not only remember events and information that pass before one, but that they also store emotional reactions to those events and the information. And, science has evidence from the testing of normal subjects that our minds have their own unique and specialized processors operating below consciousness that sift through and combine in different ways all of the information and images that are stored there. Most amazing is the brain's ability to understand itself.

It is the mind in its energy and capacity and its processing that enables a person to create poetry and music, art and sculpture, and to think, and to love. Think of your mind as having a limitless number of miniscule pigeonholes. . . little files for storing the profusion of visual images, voices and sounds heard, all of your experiences as well as everything that has past before you during your lifetime. And, so many things are stored there that are so dissimilar.

Whether standing in a crowd, sitting at a desk, or alone in a room, the eyes like an unerring camera constantly scan every object and every movement in a continuous, movie-like stream of images and information. As the eyes move about the scene, they carefully record all that passes. Everything is put down in those little file drawers in the brain from the time we get up in the morning until we go to bed at night.

At the same time we are each gathering into our personal and unique repository any sound that is heard and any kind of stimuli to our sensory systems. Nothing is truly erased from our memories except by trauma from illness or injury. Consciously or unconsciously wheresoever we may be or whatever activity we take part in, we are always recording images, sounds, and information to be held in each mind's special storeroom. Stored forever awaiting recall as well as bearing some form of influence upon our daily thoughts and behavior.

The mind might be likened to an infallible living computer far more advanced and faster than any that have been developed yet today. We know that all of the operations of our bodies and minds are powered by a labyrinthine electrical scheme. Adrian Almquist, a cardiologist with the Minneapolis Heart Institute, said that he and his colleagues are the electricians of the body. They focus upon the body's electrical system and treat people whose electrical systems have gone wrong in some way. Every bodily action or reaction is caused by electrochemical signals from the brain.

Currents inside of our bodies give us our breath of life. In order for the brain to issue its commands from neuron to neuron, it needs the power of electricity. These signals reach out to the muscles setting up electrical impulses that trigger the muscles to relax or contract. Our hearts react under a charge of electricity approximately each second. Cardiologists can chart the heart's rhythm and function by attaching about a dozen electrodes at selected points on a person's body. They record how the electrical impulses change at those points, looking for normalities or abnormalities in the heart's function.

Again, it is important to recognize, acknowledge what marvelous creations we and our children are. Each one is a distinct and separate being unlike any other. Each is building an exclusive library of especial experiences and information unlike that of any other person. Someone once said that an individual is like all others in some respects, like some others in some respects, and like no others in other respects. The thoughts and memories each person gathers and accumulates within their private well of knowledge will not be duplicated in the same way within anyone else.

The American mathematician, John von Neumann, who was honored with the Fermi Award for his work on the theory, design, and construction of computers, calculated that the human mind could store up to 280 quintillion bits of memory. That's 280,000,000,000,000,000,000 in round numbers. And, that's been viewed as a conservative figure!

Each brain will accumulate its private reservoir of knowledge and experience to be applied to whatever perplexity life may bring to its door. And, most extraordinary, each will make free choices from its reservoir, think about things that others would not think about, choose directions that are possibly not in general acceptance or based upon tradition, or follow paths of thought that haven't been taken before. All of this due to what has been unipersonally experienced in life.

Individuality is formed by that which each person is exposed to. The accumulation of experience preferably should not be gathered in a hit or miss way. From the time of birth caregivers are in the critical position of having the most meaningful influence upon the consummate growth and behavior of a child. When a mode of training places upon the child the responsibility to flail about to determine its own direction. . .left free of discipline 'in order not to suppress its creative expression' for example. . .any form of behavior may develop by chance or undirected choice. Also, a difficult or unhappy childhood, gross mistreatment and physical abuse, as well as exposure to the elements of indecency and sensuality will drive one into crime, fatalism, or sexual diversions.

No original character and personality are engraved upon one's mind at the time of their birth. Other than sensory awareness, one must gather and assemble the outward, visible aspects of character and knowledge and inventiveness from the breadth and direction of their experiences and associations.

SOME CHOOSE A HIGHROAD TO ENLIVEN
THEIR LIVES

*He who knows others is wise; he who knows himself
is enlightened.*

The way of Lao Tzu

Environment, experience and training are the bricks and mortar of intelligence and accomplishments. Each person born today does so within a world overflowing with potential to grow in mind as well as in body. Each can live their life to the fullest when moral, ethical, and social boundaries are adhered to. There are certain prescriptive guidelines that have led to achievement of purpose or making a mark in life. The most important is the preparation of the mind.

Anyone who has been successful in art or design, literature or music, constructing buildings, or even baking an epicurean pie will swear that what happens before the work actually begins is of the greatest importance. Louis Pasteur, the French chemist and microbiologist who developed the process called 'pasteurization,' said it this way, "Chance favors only the prepared mind."

An artist working in oils carefully prepares the palette before beginning work on a canvas. The artist must also know the nature and effect of the colors and their physical properties. And, should know as well such things as the mechanics of stretching a canvas properly and the different techniques of the classical and modern painters.

An architectural engineer, before planning a building project, must know what materials are available in the area and know how and when they can be delivered. It is critical that he has learned the capacity of the materials to withstand stress and wear, their composition and best functional application.

In this modern world it is necessary to gain specialized knowledge or skills to compete. We all become specialists of some kind because of the complexity and volume of information we must store in our minds. As well, we have a multiplicity of supplementary data resources which we have been educated to employ with a broad diversification of data. There are statistics and the like in text and references, and resource centers of all types. This permits us (but restricts us in one sense) to concentrate our energies within a narrow field of endeavor.

Today every field has its own requirements in background and training. The great achievers we read about in history lived in times when knowledge and its need was limited. Around 350 B.C. Artistotle had most of his writings accepted and unquestioned on natural science, logic, ethics, politics, metaphysics, poetics, and many other subjects far afield from his metier as a philosopher.

It has been said that we are all ignorant to some extent, just ignorant about different things. When we attempt to find solutions to problems in any field that may spark our interest, we must honestly ask ourselves whether or not we have the sophistication and background to successfully find answers.

There is a rule in written composition that you cannot write about anything that you haven't earned the right to write about. If not, one can supplement the limited information they have, of course, with intense research and study. But, even though research and study will provide some information, it will not substitute for actual experience.

A special performance or perfection in any field has never been the result of a moment of brilliance. More likely it was due to a lifetime of effort gathering information and experience. It had to be a curious mind and a commitment that probably found roots in childhood, and continued through schooling until realization of success. A lifetime of slowly accumulating information and becoming enlightened through trial and error before reaching their greatest accomplishment.

Successful people, morally as well as financially, tend to grow copying someone whom they admire that has mastered and gained a position in life that they have desired. What makes each of us different in our values and in the feelings we express is the result of the quality of preparation through study, associations, and unique experimentation in the different levels of our society. When people are recognized and rewarded in some way, and made to feel comfortable at a certain social level, they will clasp on to those relationships; and in this set their course in life.

There is a Chinese proverb: "A child's life is like a piece of paper upon which every passerby leaves a mark." Children have none of the practical restraints that adults have; and, soon after they enter life, begin impatiently noticing and prying. As soon as they learn to speak, they ask, "Why?. . .Where?. . .What?. . .When?. . .How?" With every question they add to their limited knowledge. As children they are eager to absorb all of the infinite variety of their new world. Sometimes they seem almost desperate searching for answers among all of the puzzles in their young lives.

The preparation of each individual begins early, and there is a struggle to sort out the influences faced, the learning opportunities accessible, and to self-evaluate one's abilities. We are all travelers on the road of life; and in our travels we will have many adventures and opportunities to learn and to fill our private wells of knowledge.

Brilliance of mind, moral social attitudes, and achievement are bred from environment as well as education. But for the most part from the experiences in our lives. The degree of brilliance or moral social attitudes will correlate directly with the breadth, nature, and quality of a person's experiences, associations, and cultural background.

Regrettably we become creatures of convention readily accepting what is comfortable and not challenging. We can become adhered to the routines and behavior of friends and associates. It is never too late to attempt a makeover of the organized and set pattern of one's behavior and interests, and one can regain the burning curiosity that was characteristic as a child. And, by that reenergize interest in the world's wonders and mysteries.

Thomas Huxley wrote, "The world is as fresh as it was at the first day, and as full of untold novelties for him who has the eyes to see them." A sense that anything is possible, the feeling that there are more interesting things in the world than it is possible to try or view, can build ethics and morality into a person's life.

An uneventful or jejune way of living can be broken by striving each day to try some new activity, converse with someone new, learn some extra bit of knowledge, to observe something not seen or experienced before. There are ways one can develop in oneself a child's aptitude for making desirable discoveries by accident. To discover a limitless variety of self-starting and rewarding experiences leaves no room for transgression and will set ethical and moral boundaries for people and those around them. Open to everyone is an array of possible channels to expose and explore the world we live in.

Changing habitual activities for some that are new and unfamiliar might bring challenges and offer some fearsome frontiers. Like placing yourself in a certain amount of danger. It does suit some very well. Try traveling to a country in conflict or troubled.

Ask yourself to develop a bold inquisitiveness and concern about what other people are doing. . .thrust yourself into other people's affairs if this may please you. Search out things to view that have not been common in your pattern or life or life style. You may have never been to a live ballet performance. If one is within easy reach, you'll find that no other athletic event requires so much muscular power and endurance and such perfected skills and grace. It is an experience that will certainly reward you.

There are those who have never bothered to visit an art, history, or natural science museum; or a zoo or marine exhibit. These are places to discover and appreciate new information, and satisfy the mind's curiosity. The loss is only a few hours out of a day that could be frittered away anyway.

Many people overlook a myriad of theatrical events each year that can be reached by car or even the bus. Series tickets can be purchased that will bring pleasant and rewarding experiences to look forward to throughout the coming months that broaden one's vistas.

The role of spectator can be a worthwhile exercise (on the scene and not gluing oneself to a television set for Monday night sports). If leaving a confining family room and bodily attending a sports event has been foreign in your pattern of life, try as

84

many types as you can handle. . .at least once. . .take the kids or someone else along with you, of course. But be sure to make an honest attempt to understand the fundamentals and rules of the game.

As a person adds to their reservoir of memories in this way, it expands their understanding of the world around them. If you have ever caught yourself saying, "Oh, we never go to the movies," you are missing out on great entertainment. New releases of great interest are being issued constantly with a diversity of drama, mystery, and comedy. Pamper your ego by being able to say that you have seen all of those popular and of merit that are current. Consider them carefully though because many are overly sexual, overly violent, or just plain bad. Ask someone who may have already seen them, or consult the critics' reviews. You will find many acceptable providing pleasure, satisfaction, and enlightenment. And, then there are discount places where even the popcorn is reasonable.

There are many who actively and feverishly participate in sports. . .this is fine if it is only a part of very broad interests. There is excitement and competition engaging in a sport yourself. It can do amazing things for one's health and stamina while remaining within any physical limitations. Everyone should be engaged in something physical anyway be it tennis, golf, soccer, archery, or whatever turns you on. There is plenty of professional support for training the beginners as well as those with advanced skills.

Have you ever had a creative urge to draw or paint? There can be much satisfaction gained from enrollment in classes to nurture this noble part of our culture. Winston Churchill the statesman, Tony Bennett the singer, and many among the busy rich and famous have excelled in oil painting and other artistic undertakings for expansion of their lives and their relaxation. Don't be afraid to copy. Student artists spend a lot of time copying plaster casts and classic paintings as a required step in their training. Gaugin, Renoir, all of the master painters spent hours copying the work of the master painters that preceded them while they were developing their own skills.

Mary Cassatt, for example, the only female accepted by the

'Impressionist' group of painters, was frustrated by her early training in the tedious but common method of drawing from plaster casts of famous sculptors. However, she remained steadfast in her belief that copying was the best and only method for training in technique, and advised all young student artists to be self-schooled by this method.

Try acting if you dare! There are many little theaters around. . .amateur as well as the professional. It is usually not too difficult to find a cast to join nearby at a church or school or club. And, how about singing? You might try joining a chorus or church choir. They are usually looking for new members of any age.

Often some have an itch to take lessons on piano or maybe some other instrument. You know schools encourage students to involve themselves in the band or orchestra as one of the basics of education. Matthew Green, the English poet, wrote, "Music hath charms, we all may find, ingratiate deeply with the mind." Your well of experience would be shallow indeed if it did not include an appreciation for a variety of music forms. Jack Benny loved the violin and played publicly, though he could never challenge the skills of Ole Bull.

Francis Bacon said, "Travel, in the younger sort, is a part of education; in the elder, a part of experience." There have never been so many opportunities for anyone to see the country or see the world. Of course, the maps of Europe and Asia change shape and dimension by the minute, and it is necessary to review places of exploration in advance for safety's sake. Strike out on your own whenever you are able, traveling like the locals do, and seek out community gatherings and local hangouts. Luxury resorts and cruises are certainly pleasurable and an easy way to go. When there is someone you can visit in their homeland abroad, such as relatives or friends, it can be much more enjoyable and rewarding.

But travel can be as simple as short jaunts by car or bus to a town or place nearby never visited before. A drive on a Sunday to some out-of-the-way place can also be diverting and entertaining. My wife and I have tried some of the country inns for an overnight. We have also found it refreshing to drive out to a church dinner in one of the small towns on a weekend meeting friendly folk and having a generously satisfying meal. There were new personalities to meet and to stimulate conversazione. Or, take walks alone as well as with friends or family, and peer into other peoples windows if you want to. You don't have to travel far to find some stimulation for your curiosity.

The advantages of reading, of course, are manifold. One should subscribe to at least 10 to 20 of the popular magazines published. It is not necessary to read every page of the publications from top to bottom. Scan through looking for highlights, things of special interest to you. Also, read newspapers from other cities, say the New York Times, slanted to their own environment, giving an encyclopedic view of what's happening there and the tenor of the populace. It 's almost like living there.

Public libraries are free of charge and easily accessible today. They are often overlooked as a rich resource not only for information but for entertainment. They have trained librarians who are eager to assist in finding interesting subjects and books. A person can become educated in new fields of interest. How about the classic great books? Bacon, Milton, Thucydides, Aristotle, and others? I found when experimenting with ancient literature you may have to plod through them at first, but they are filled with interesting philosophies that will fit modern times situations. There are surprising references now and then to events and individuals in history. You will find there recorded happenings and some individuals in religious history that are interesting.

Getting into some of these new experiences or altering behavior patterns can be like deliberately acquiring tastes for new and different kinds of foods and drinks. By the way, that can be a fruitful change of behavior as well. Like to cook, bake, or brew? The subject of food is dear to all of us. You know, of course, there are home economists and chemists in food development who have made a rewarding occupation out of that activity. Others, for purely personal enjoyment, experiment with different recipes and combinations of ingredients, and explore the world of culinary arts for new and exciting tastes.

Volunteering for a worthy cause will provide its own rewards. Public service in education, environmental programs or community service, excites some into spending at least a little time doing something for the public good. They gain a good feeling about themselves, and present a model for others to follow their lead.

We can change what we do and think about to our advantage in life. Though clinging to past patterns of behavior, of course, is easy, predictable, and safe. I attended a class reunion recently. Some of my former classmates had not changed a wink over the years. The same activities, the same clothes, the same hair treatment, etc. But there were some who had really changed and blossomed into new and interesting people. I hope that I have changed. Touched by the many experiences that curiosity had led them to, it had added to their lives and their appearance. They had gained a little more of this or that.

It would be humanly impossible for anyone to attempt to become involved in all of these changes in their behavior patterns. Also, one might get stiffening resistance from friends, family, or associates. But, as Goethe wrote, "One ought, every day at least, to hear a little song, read a good poem, see a fine picture; and, if it were possible, to speak a few reasonable words."

VISIONS ROOTED IN SOLITUDE

It is the lone worker who makes the first advance in a subject; the details may be worked out by a team, but the prime idea is due to the enterprise, thought, and perception of an individual.

Sir Alexander Fleming

Albert Einstein's celebrated achievement, his theory of relativity, was accomplished by a single scientist working alone and out of the academic mainstream. As a child he was said to be shy, lonely and withdrawn from the world. His teachers said that he was mentally slow, unsociable and adrift forever in his foolish dreams. He once wrote, "I live in that solitude which is painful in youth, but delicious in years of maturity."

Each human being faces a different world of their own. What we become is formed by the variety of things experienced. This will shape each character and his or her behavior. The lives of exceptional achievers often will show them absorbed in the silent processing within the subconscious mind as it reacts to the inner thoughts of the conscious mind. This concentrated thinking favors solitude and quiescence. Many have been known to be almost completely rapt in their own thoughts even in company.

The most marvelous thing about the subconscious mind is its role as an infinitely deep resource of information from experiences and exposure to all sorts of knowledge and images. The mind becomes a huge personal reference library with omniscient powers to apply this information interdependently toward a suitable end. It can process the profusion of reading, talking, listening, and viewing in one's background; and then present the conscious mind with new and profitable combinations of information. A process of sorting and comparing new experiences with the past. and arranging many of the experiences in its file of the past into new visions for the future. And, all of this must take place in seclusion before it is displayed in the open.

An example of this pattern of sequestration is the life of Helen Beatrix Potter. This writer of children's books in the world of Peter and Flopsy and Mopsy Cottontail spent most of her childhood without any companionship except for a variety of rabbits, mice, hedgehogs, etc. collected on walks around their country estate in Scotland, and which she kept as pets. She didn't attend school, and, outside of her brother, had little chance for the company of other children. She was very shy. In spite of this she became famous for her storybooks written in her seclusive life, publishing the first herself. She became well-known for her studies of animals and insects.

The intricate processing within our minds may never be understood completely, but in an examination of the lives of the recognized composers, writers, painters, sculptors, and other achievers of the past or present it is evident that the processing requires time without distraction, a preference for solitude to work their wonders. Edward Gibbon, the English historian of the 18th century, wrote, "Conversation enriches the understanding, but solitude is the school of genius." And his life reflected this.

Michel Eyguem de Montaigne, whose essays were considered the highest expression of the 16th century French prose, wrote, "A man should keep for himself a little back shop, all his own, quite unadulterated, in which he establishes his true freedom and chief place of seclusion and solitude." Children at some point in their early lives should be given favorable time, moments of golden privacy in which their imaging power, castle-building and fanciful dreaming will be cultivated to blossom and ripen. This to offer a secure place or space of understood limits when the need seems to be asked or pursued.

Such a quiet time should never be imposed but provided. A time for reading or listening to music or whatever. For children this is a time away from other children, away from adult chaperonage. Don't look upon the desire to be alone as an escape. There must remain, of course, a secure place for a child to return to out of its seclusion.

Peace and solitude are difficult to come by in this hurly-burly world of ours. We are apt to involve ourselves as well as our families in an endurance trial of activities and events that never include periods of time away from social distractions. The desire and the ability to be alone is really a sign of the growth of emotional maturity.

On the other hand, though inventive and reflective thought is an intimate and private thing necessary for full growth of the mind, the value of interaction with others should never be minimized or given no heed. It is the school for learning social skills necessary for confidence and self-realization. As well, as adults we find that open discussion and exchange of our views with others helps us escape from imposed patterns in our lives and misdirection of thought.

We know when one explains a problem or considered solutions for a problem with some other person or persons, whether or not they have command of the field or subject you are exploring, one will find it necessary to fully clarify and amplify one's assumptions and position. This helps to break away from any conditioning one may have fallen victim to by not fully analyzing their thoughts and discoveries up to that point. W. I. B. Beveridge said in 'The Art of Scientific Investigation,' "not infrequently it happens that while one is making the explanation a new thought occurs to one without the person having said a word.

I find the same may happen during the delivery of a lecture, for when the teacher explains something, he 'sees' it more clearly himself than he had before. The other persons asking questions, even ill-informed ones, may make the narrator break the established chain. . .it disturbs the settled arrangement and brings about new combinations."

When we sweat over a problem, our line of thought can become firmly established as we work at our problem. Our thoughts are conditioned to the first direction of our thinking, and the chain is difficult to break. An open discussion with anyone will make it necessary to clearly explain the position on a problem. This aids in avoiding being led down a false trail in the thought process.

On the flip side, group thinking in open discussions can sometimes have a negative result. One person may dominate the reasoning or reflection of the group, and channel the thoughts and conclusions of the other participants. In an open forum there can be a fear of being wrong or risking ridicule for a particular viewpoint or line of reasoning. There is a tendency to follow the lead-thinking of someone eloquent or forceful.

People who have shown unusual inventive thinking and skills often are individualists. They have accomplished their best work alone and have required a certain amount of isolation in which to express and evaluate the products of their thoughts or skills. They can anticipate and be sensitive to premature criticism that could destroy or alter their ideas before they could be completely formulated.

Such is the fact that a jury can be directed in its verdict by the strength of one person on the panel. 'Putting heads together' to solve problems so often will fail. Each individual has had a unique set of experiences in life, and each has a composition of solitary characteristics and knowledge qualitatively different from everyone else.

During the early forties an advertising agency created and promoted 'brainstorming' as the answer for everything from boring advertising to unsaleable products. Creative staff were gathered together with one person acting as a monitor to record whatever issued from the group. A problem would be placed on the table for everyone to consider. They were urged to shout out any idea or thought that came to mind associated with the problem presented to them. They were asked to let the words flow out without censor or judgment. The accumulation of the thoughts and ideas that were recorded would be evaluated for the best of the ideas from such a session, and then one or more would be selected for formal presentation.

Such sessions surfaced differing points of view and opinions from a variety of personalities and differences in their background experiences that resulted in a lot of useless material and compromises of conclusions. In more recent years a similar exercise has become known as a 'think tank.' As Sir Alexander Fleming, the Scottish bacteriologist and the Nobel Prize winner for the discovery and development of penicillin, said, ". . .details may be worked out by a team, but the prime idea is due to the enterprise, thought and perception of an individual."

Of course in television shows and similar presentations, teams of writers must be used because of the volume of material that must be assembled within a very short time period. In such productions there must always be a lead writer who will direct and weave a 'golden thread' into the forming of the production. This is the concept from the single mind that will flow throughout the production.

In the popular soap theaters there is a principal star writer at the helm who will plan and write the main story line and characters. This may be the basis for the script for as much as a year ahead. A team of 'breakdown writers' do the labor of outlining each of the episodes and summarizing what will be accomplished in each scene. 'Dialogue writers,' suited to the personality of each role in the show, will write the actual words to be spoken in the scenes.

Each of the writers, of course, make their separate contributions to enhance the performance under the watchful scrutiny of the lead writer. No matter what, actor participants may each draw from their own unique experience to exhibit originality brought about by their own acting skills. On the stage or in a screenplay, although the work may have been presented many times before, the director and each actor may bring something exciting and original to its performance. This is true as well in a musical work, which may be a masterpiece in itself but may be enhanced and made new again by the skill of the performers or the director.

From the time of their birth to their maturity the extended period of time spent learning from their parents or caregivers may be one quarter or more of a child's lifespan. And it must include times of self-enjoyment away from others and away from close supervision. The experience of being alone brings with it self-discovery and self-realization. Hidden in each day of our lives are small precious moments like nuggets of gold in a stream just waiting to be discovered, removed with care, clarified and formed into something of beauty for ourselves alone.

NEVER, NEVER THROW ANYTHING AWAY

I usually have a heap of preliminary papers close at hand during the writing. Scribbled notes, memory props in part purely objective. . .external details, colorful odds and ends. . .also psychological formulations, and fragmentary inspirations, which I use in their proper place

Thomas Mann, *Nobel Prize winner in literature*

Much like the muscles of the body, the brain changes with its experience. It molds and remodels itself to fit the world around it, to associations and relationships. What we become will be formed from our experiences in living and the impressions and knowledge carved in our memories.

The ability to retrieve information from our well of memories is a learned skill. A capacity for brilliance and creativity is dependent upon a faculty for gathering the information and images from the mind to be combined for solutions to the problems that are faced. The fusion of past experiences with the present is necessary in the evolution of a reasoning mind, and to maintain a steadfast and socially passable human behavior.

Whatever is needed to solve problems, answer tough questions, or erect barriers to miscreant behavior can usually be located somewhere in our memories. Memories that may be fading but not erased, simply misfiled. Throughout our lives the brain receives, stores, and processes more information at an unconscious level than at the conscious level. It is known that the subconscious part of the mind that stores this information will interact with the conscious mind to guide perception, judgment, and behavior.

It is the ability to retrieve experiences and images from that vast repository of the mind for each new purpose that will support our inventive, problem-solving thoughts. Wolfgang Amadeus Mozart, an Austrian musician who composed over 600 profound works unexcelled in beauty, said that he took his ideas out of the bag of his memories that he had collected previously.

Some of those into scientific experimental investigation believe that memory decays with the passing of time. Some theorize that newer information will block out older information stored, thus making older information difficult to retrieve. It is true, of course, that as we age we are apt to shut many things out of our lives and memories, and give attention only to our concerns of the moment. For example, elderly people can skillfully recall meaningful information that is current and directly affecting their lives; but they will discard information or memories on subjects that are no longer important or of concern to them.

Children are eager to see and experience everything around them, eager to fill the bottomless capacity of their empty young minds with information. During that early period in their lives curiosity and ambitions are at a fever pitch. The recall of all of the fresh material that is new in their experience is accomplished with little difficulty. Though children may also experience the fading of some memories of things that do not peak their interest. Though missing, memories continue to exist. . .they have not left the library of the mind.

In the busy, crowded world in which we live today most memory failures are the result of the lack of concentration. It is difficult to concentrate on certain issues or subjects because of the hysteria of the lives around us. There is a constant press of new information from so many sources that is overwhelming.

Today the lack of concentration, hyperactivity, and short attention span in our children has been formally labeled as an 'attention deficit disorder.' It is a condition leading to learning disabilities and behavioral problems. It is precipitated and propelled by an environment of frantic, disorderly haste and overactivity that is generated in many households. The golden moments of solitude that can be set aside as suggested earlier in this book are therapeutic moments to slow down and regain circumspection and restraint. Some time away and alone by oneself is necessary.

In this age it is normal and commonplace to take on too

many activities and agonize over how to possibly race fast enough to complete everything that we think we need to accomplish or participate in. As a result we place much of the information that we consciously or unconsciously absorb in some dark place in our minds that becomes difficult to retrieve.

Whatever will interfere with our attention will interfere with our conscious retention of information. We often build a wall or shield in defense against the mass of messages that are directed at us, though many of these messages must be absorbed subconsciously.

There are many teaching methods offered for improving memory, better described as 'memory aids.' There are mnemonic devices that help people to remember things. The term 'mnemonic' comes from the name Mnemosyne, the Greek goddess of memory. These are memory aid methods that can be logical or crazy, complex or very simple. Mnemonic tricks are behind the amazing performances that you may have seen by memory experts appearing on the stage or on television programs. Those who teach courses in memory improvement use mnemonic devices in their techniques. The most common ones use a train of associations serving as clues to remembering things.

As adults our experiences and the images in our minds continue to accumulate and somewhere along the line an information overload sets in. It is then that it may require some schematization of a sort to help bring sidetracked information back from the past.

At one time I took great pleasure in one of the mnemonic tricks, and I used it often at parties to dazzle my friends. I would tell them that I could memorize an entire deck of cards. It really was a simple trick but confounding for my audience.

In secret beforehand, I arranged the deck according to the following sentence: "The 62nd (the six and the deuce) infantry (an ace) beat the 93rd (nine and a trey) and the king's (a king, of course) 8 thousand and 4 men (an eight, ten, four, and a jack) and 75 women (the seven, a five and a queen)."

All of the cards in the deck were arranged in this order alternating the suits from one card to the next starting with a spade, then a diamond, a club, and a heart. This order was repeated over and over again throughout the deck of cards. I then riffled the deck for show (a short, coarse shuffling does not seem to disturb the order too much), and had someone select a card from the center of the deck. I then cut the deck at the same place in the deck where the selected card was withdrawn. . .then I sneaked a peek at the card next to the one withdrawn and could identify the card the person held.

These mnemonic devices have their place and can be very effective in memorizing points or subjects to be covered in a speech. They are a simple means of remembering lists of any kind when it is difficult to use simple repetition to commit something to memory. Some of these devices use association as a tool to remember names of contacts in business or social groups. Mental visualization is also used linking things with common objects, such as rooms in a house, to help in remembering lists of things.

There certainly are practical uses for some of these devices or tricks. The salesman, for example, and the pastor of a church, those who rely on an ability to remember the names of customers, parishoners, etc., can become very skilled in recalling names through these association devices. However, these methods will not make it possible to retain the mass of information we are exposed to in our day to day lives. These mnemonic devices will not serve us in searching the mind for all of the experiences, images, and other information buried there.

How best to make the trip to the attic of the past? How to make an exhaustive investigation within the mind's well of experience and information?

There is a method for bringing to consciousness the information stored in the subconscious mind that can possibly be combined in the construction of solutions to problems or the forming of productive ideas.

We are not limited to fixing things in memory only through mnemonics or repetitious exercises. There is another method for capturing information and images out of the depths of the subconscious mind. For a simple illustration of this, have you ever attended a workshop or seminar where experts have been invited to teach their specialties? These events can last for a few hours or even a few days. They are required by many business firms or other commercial organizations for continuing education. This is especially true in licensed or certified occupational categories. There are educational workshops that can be attended by anyone who feels the need for further education in some activity or subject.

Normally you arrive at the appointed time and place and are seated. You are given an outline of the program and possibly some take-home materials for later reference. You may choose to take notes or just sit throughout the seminar simply as a serious listener. It comes to an end and you hurry back to the office or to your home. The seminar materials and notes are tossed into a desk drawer or file, and you go about your business as usual.

Then some weeks later, maybe when someone asked about the seminar, you would probably be unable to remember clearly, if at all, the title or the subject of the workshop, names of the presenters, and much less all of the salient points raised during the workshop. Very little remaining of a subject that was clearly in your memory only a short time before, even though you may have been very much impressed by it and felt you had gained much from the seminar.

One day some weeks or months later you are sitting idly planning what you should do next. You reach into that desk drawer or file and discover the notes taken and materials received at the seminar. While scanning the material there immediately flashes before you the subject, persons who presented, and those good points you may have carefully recorded in your notes or were printed in your take-home materials.

Some information fades from your memory as time passes because it has no important place in the current focus of your interests. Because you have no immediate need for the information, it may seem unnecessary to engrave it in your memory. But, recall of any information is easy if you have a ready reference file or journal to bring the information back into your consciousness whenever you have a need for it.

Often the name of someone will escape us when we need it most. It is something on the tip of your tongue but only hangs there seeming to be irretrievable. Hopefully someone will offer a clue or there is a list of names handy for quick reference. When a given clue works or a list of names helps you to retrieve the name you hoped to remember, you will very likely form an image in your mind of that person. You will fill in many details about the person that seemed to be missing forever before. Memories that come to us easily are taken for granted without serious thought. We notice only when our memory fails us.

Professional creative people. . .writers, artists, and musicians. . .seem better equipped to marshal broad patterns of memories. They are organized for gathering, recognizing, and embracing the information they need to do the work before them. Everyone knows that writing things down helps us to remember things.

We often take notes and make lists of things. I have observed that most all of the skilled creative people I have known have been veritable magpies. These were people who saved and stored everything and anything.

All professional writers or artists that I have worked with or have known have had in some form what we have called a 'swipe file.' In spite of what this term may imply, this is not for the purpose of plagiarizing ideas. It may be a space in a desk or cabinet. It could be some old cartons stashed in a storeroom, or on shelving in an office. Or, it may be an attractive, efficient, steel office file cabinet with many carefully prepared folders clearly labeled with subjects.

Regardless of whether the swipe file would be rated as good or bad housekeeping, it is stuffed with clippings from newspapers, magazines, and other publications. They are kept because they hold some special interest for the owner of the file. You would find slips of paper with handwritten stray thoughts, whole articles on curious subjects, and many things that may have caught the attention and were dropped into the file.

A swipe file could have many pictures and things that would remind one of especially good or unusual experiences, or things useful in the owners work or occupation. I have seen artists that

100

have kept pictures of hands, feet, boats, animals, and almost anything of possible value for use in future renderings. Incidentally, have you ever noticed when you see a photograph of an author that he will be posed most often in front of shelves loaded with books of every description (his swipe file).

These are not only collections of things from recent experiences and observations but collections from the long, fading past as well. This is a place throughout a lifetime or career where things of special interest to only that one person have been secretly and intimately gathered. Reminders of events and experiences in the past remembered at some later time and used to advantage in some way.

As one leafs through all of the articles, pictures, etc. in the swipe file, flipping carelessly through momentos of images, emotions, enlightenments, and data from life's encounters of the past, they are carried back in clear and complete recollection. One can skim through the swipe file (actually a journal) sailing over the collection until something is spotted that may reflect upon a problem or task being pursued, and then swoop down upon it.

Never, never throw anything away, especially things akin to those vestigial tokens from your past. It could become the loss of a bit of your life. You could be closing the door on some knowledge or experience buried in your past in your subconscious mind. And, it could have been used to unravel a knotty problem you might face tomorrow.

It can be helpful to note on any item or piece of material dropped into the swipe file (it could also be called a diary or journal) a date and maybe where you happened upon the material and what prompted you to save it. This aids one when musing over the material to resurface the situation or conditions at the time it was dropped into the file. Thus this swipe file, journal, or diary is preserving experiences, information, and events in a person's life that can be recalled from memories again and again.

Everyone should be encouraged to keep such a journal or diary to record events to be enjoyed later in their lives. A place to collect memories, not to be filed and forgotten, but to be explored in their resurrection for application to problems arising in the future or to relive emotions.

Memories resurface when stimulated in some way. Sometimes simply by a remark someone might make about a past event. Being in certain surroundings, a certain setting, under special conditions, influences or circumstances. Anything that will shake the senses will excite a wave of recall of experiences in the past.

For anyone old enough, on a clear fall night when temperatures are crisp you can almost smell burning leaves and feel the warmth of a bonfire (now outlawed in most communities). Maybe as well, the taste of marshmallows or wieners cooking over the fire. A turkey, goose, or ham roasting in the oven or other rich, pleasantly odorous foods simmering on the stove will bring back the elation and spirit of a Thanksgiving, Christmas, Easter, or other holiday past with family and friends jubilating. Recognizing, of course, these experiences can be a link as well to unpleasant things of the past. . .someone missed, better days longed for, or some other time of want.

My father was a painter and wallpaper decorator, and the odor of paint or wallpaper paste never fails to bring back pictures of my brother and I climbing ladders, scraping walls, doing the many tasks father required when we had time to spare. He always smoked cigars. The smell of fireworks immediately brings a flashback of the time the ashes of his cigar fell into a sack of pyrotechnics in his arms purchased at a roadside stand at the Fourth of July celebration. This was just as we were leaving to return to our car. . .along with the jumping, the flailing of hands and arms, and shouting.

For some the smell of a wood fire in a potbellied stove and warm, wet clothing on a chilly day is a reminder of skating on a frozen pond with friends. There were games and childhood romances, and resting on a bench in a warming house.

Even the unpleasant stench of farm animals and greasy foods cooking awakes memories for some of a State Fair, the midway rides, and displays of arts and crafts. The smell of freshly mowed grass, gasoline, or freshly caught fish brings to my mind outings when I was young. Not only smelling, but also touching, tasting, hearing certain things can bring vivid recall of experiences pleasantly warming as well as those that are disquieting.

Nothing is ever truly forgotten. I and others I have talked to on this subject have had things flash back into the conscious mind long, long after the experience had passed and supposedly forgotten. At the time they happened they could not have seemed to be of real value and tagged for 'short term' or 'long term' storage in memory. When they resurfaced, they were then embellished with more detail than one could have ever imagined.

When we recall something from the past, we can picture in our mind a reflection of the complete likeness of a person or object. We then consider the particular parts of the likeness for answers to our questions about it. Whenever the likeness seems incomplete, it is our creative nature to fill missing details into the image in our mind. These may be elements we expect or want to be part of that image. Picture that new dress or that new car, and you can paint-in more details in your mind's eye as surely as though you had a brush in hand.

It is helpful while researching your mind for information, to keep pad and pencil handy to carefully record and describe what you have envisioned. Buy a small notebook and carry it with you. Write down whatever stray thoughts that may come to you. This is something that Einstein, Faraday, and most of the famous thought provokers would do always. This keeps thoughts and visions in control as you search your conscious and subconscious memory. . .trapping fading thoughts or images before they fade away again.

Out of those pigeonholes in the mind, out of a labyrinth of memories, we can bring forward most all of the information needed for the solutions to questions.

This is a system of constructing useful combinations through selections from your journal, diary, or swipe file. Experience will tell one when to grasp a memory or when to let it go. Great care must be taken in the preservation of the mementos of the past. Georg Christoph Lichtenberg, a German physicist and satirist in the eighteenth century, expressed it this way: "There is something in our minds like sunshine and weather which is not under our control. When I write, the best things come to me from I know not where."

Memory in the human animal is more than storage of images, thoughts, information, and sensations. There is also something else that you will recognize. I have called it 'muscle memory.' At some time in our youth, with some struggle, we usually learn to ride a bicycle. Giving it a try some years later, after a lengthy absence from bike riding, we find we still have the balance and some of the skill to ride one. This is our muscle memory.

Special skills that have been learned, the smooth trained swing with a golf club, the flow of the serve with a tennis racket, the message to the legs to clear a high hurdle, the unerring strike of a carpenter's hammer, the rapid finger stroking of the keys of a computer or typewriter keyboard. . .they are also filed in those minute pigeon holes in the mind. Training and practice have put them there.

After long periods of disuse, such skills can often be reclaimed, barring illness or trauma. Though somewhat clumsily at first, former skills can be recovered in much the same way that information and images can be reclaimed from the mind's treasury of memories.

Habits formed early in life through experience both in skills and behavior will remain with a person throughout life unless altered with therapy or a determined will. The first sexual encounter for a boy or girl, if homosexual in nature. . .consensual, seduced, or abusively. . .is 60 percent likely to be followed by an ongoing homosexual attraction according to studies by research psychologist Paul Cameron. As well he said studies by pro-homosexual researchers show that 25 percent of gay men admit that, when they were over 21, they had had sex with boys under 16 years old.

Children begin life with an unrelenting curiosity. They have an amazing fervor to explore the worlds that are held open for them. When the answers to their questions and correct information are withheld or ignored, the fervor of their curiosity will stray. Nurtured carefully with discipline and strict rules of conduct, the quality of their behavior will remain with them throughout their lives.

WE SEE ONLY WHAT WE KNOW

The senses of seeing and hearing may be cultivated and trained as well as the sense of touch. But to find what you are looking for, to catch the sly winks and gestures on every side, to see all the by-play going on around you, missing no significant note or movement, penetrating every screen with your eyebeams. . .that is to be an observer; that is to have an eye practiced like a blind man's touch.

John Burroughs, *the American Naturalist*

We acquire much of our information observing people and the world about us. It is the listening, seeing, touching, tasting, and scenting firsthand. What a person actually sees or senses in any way provides assurance and confidence in the truth-value of any of the information we gather. Our skill in observing activity, sensations, sounds, and objects within our element also has a direct bearing on the knowledge we acquire or the behavior we accept or the opportunities we embrace.

If our attention only turns to those things we expect to see, we will probably overlook the unexpected. Some give their attention only to the things that relate to their personal, narrow interests and pass by any others. As Goethe, the German poet said, "We see only what we know."

W.I.B. Beveridge, the biologist researcher in his 'The Art of Scientific Investigation, wrote, "People viewing the same scene will notice different things.

In a country scene a botanist will notice the different species of plants, a zoologist the animals, a geologist the geological structures, a farmer the crops and farm animals. A city dweller with none of these interests may see only a pleasant scene. Most men can pass a day in the company of a woman, and afterwards have only the vaguest idea about the clothes she wore, but most women after meeting another woman for only a few minutes could describe every article the other was wearing."

In spite of all of the reported successes of neuroscience, very little is known today about what takes place in the cerebral hemispheres. Most likely the source of mental brilliance will be found in that vast repository of chance or arranged happenings registered from experiences in life. Our individual makeup is surely dependent upon where our curiosity, associations, and impressions lead us.

John Locke, the English philosopher famous for his writings on the nature of knowledge, said, "The human mind begins as a blank slate and acquires knowledge through the use of the five senses and a process of reflection. No man's knowledge here can go beyond his experience."

Faculties of insight and creativeness can be increased by following the example of the behavior patterns of the exceptional achievers of the past. They have been voracious readers, and worked fixedly to absorb, assimilate, and store a broad diversity of experiences. It was said that Louis Pasteur when dining with friends, to their consternation, would examine their hands, the tablecloth, peer at a crumb of bread to see its form and character.

They also have had a habit of gathering information and learning facts from everyone's point of view whether or not it was in conflict with their own. They searched libraries and endless sources for information, seeking out and associating with people who had knowledge in the particular subjects they pursued. They took notes religiously, weighed and considered carefully all of the data they gathered.

The skill of being observant in everything one does and everywhere one goes can be learned by disciplining oneself to be observing, with practice and there are exercises. It can become a habit. Critical observation is the habit of looking at everything, and speculating about the causes and results of everything. To be all observant is to be continually trying to detect all possible sights, sounds, smells, textures, movements, ideas and meanings. There is also formal training.

At one time I was enrolled in a class in writing while attending George Washington University. We were required to take an examination at the end of the course that proved to be an excellent exercise in critical observation. A classroom of normal size, with the usual furnishings of tables, desks, chairs, and other school paraphernalia, had been prepared in advance. The professor had added a clutter of dozens and dozens of objects of different sizes, shapes, and materials. The clutter was displayed haphazardly throughout the room. . .on the tables and desks, on chairs, and on the walls. The class was divided into separate groups of students who were asked in turn to enter the room for a set period of time to observe and remember as much as they could without notes or any other aid to memory.

The first reaction upon entering was to take an overall look at the room. There were round and square shaped and irregularly formed things. There were familiar articles one could easily identify, but many thingumabobs you might not recognize. There was a hodgepodge of colors, not only in solid designs but many were detailed or patterned. Most of the items were stationary but some were in motion.

We had been cautioned not to miss the ordinary, accepted objects that might be taken for granted and easily overlooked. For example, the clock on the wall. common to all of the classrooms. As well the desks and other expected, normal appurtenances.

The weather was very warm as I recall. There was a fan in the corner of the room moving back and forth stirring some of the stuff on the tables. A window was open to the street outside with hanging sheer drapes that billowed out into the room because of the breeze coming through the window. I still recall there were people passing by on the cement walkway outside of the building. Through the window one could see other buildings and retail stores. There were city workers in the street with trucks and equipment and many cars and some buses.

Among the many things awaiting notice in the room were sounds of different kinds. A metronome on one table was tapping out a rhythmic beat. There was a loud tick-tocking of the clock on the wall, humming blades of the fan in the corner, the cars outside, the buses, and there was the footsteps of the passersby on the walk. A police siren was heard in the distance. These sounds competed with those from the other students in the room. . .muffled voices and shuffling feet.

Then there were small vials of liquids on the table for

tasting, smelling, or whatever. Little saucers held different kinds of stuff. Some smelled pleasant, and some were acrid and burned the nose, or were simply offensive. It was the time of the year when the shrubs outside of the open window were blooming and they had a sweet, welcome scent.

The odors mingled with the smell of the exhaust from the cars and diesel trucks in the street. And, you could not miss the hygienic odor from the freshly oiled and polished floors in the room that are common to a school. I noticed that some of the materials draped on the chairs smelled musty, and there was an odor of mothballs.

There were edible things in some of the dishes on the tables. . .bits of colored candies, cookies, small squares of cake, some sauces along with other things that could be tasted by the students. Some of these things were sweet and pleasant, others were sour and tart. There were things in dishes you could not identify. It took courage to taste some of the mixtures because of their foul appearance; but, to complete the exercise successfully, we had to try them if only with a touch of the finger to the tongue.

Everything in that room called for some examination with touching. Some things were smooth and satinlike, others felt coarse and rough to sandy. There were textures of the furs and metals, wood, and cloth. There were creamy, fatty, syrupy, and gummy things. The guard hairs on the furs felt somewhat coarse and stiff while the underfur was soft as silk. Some things felt moist and some very dry. There were objects that felt warm and there were others that were cool to the touch.

There was a breeze coming through the window. . .gently cool but raising goose flesh on bare arms. At the same time the sun's rays streaming through the upper part of the window felt pleasantly warm on the face. As well in such close quarters, one could feel the movement of the bodies of the other students as they squeezed by among the tables.

The time limit finally expired and the door to the room was opened. Each group of students returned to their regular classroom. There they were asked to write down all of the things observed, and to describe each thing as carefully and accurately as they were able for the ratings.

Through this exercise we were actually introduced to the very nature of a curious mind, and the importance of noticing and critically observing everything happening in the world around us. Sir Thomas Browne, the English physician in his widely translated 'Religio Medici,' wrote, "Not wrung from speculations and subtleties, but from common sense and observation. . .not picked from the leaves of any author, but bred amongst the weeds and tares of mine own brain."

While observing a particular subject, one will so often discover interesting and pertinent information about another subject along the way. As Sir Winston Churchill said, "Most men stumble over great discoveries, and most men then pick themselves up and walk away (from them).

Consider these precepts for an insightful, observant and inventive mind:

Do more than just see, examine

Do more than just listen, understand

Do more than just taste, savor

Do more than just smell, discern

Do more than just touch, feel

Do more than just read, question

SUBCONSCIOUS MINDS WORK MAGIC IN PAUSAL INTERLUDE

". . .when the manuscript had lain in a pigeonhole two years, I took it out one day and read the last chapter I had written. It was then that I made the great discovery that when the tank runs dry you've only to leave it alone and it will fill up again in time, while you are asleep. . .also while you are at work at other things and quite unaware that this unconscious and profitable celebration is going on. There was plenty of material now and the book went on and finished itself without any trouble.

Mark Twain *(speaking of the writing of 'Tom Sawyer')*

Have you ever owned or maybe seen a kaleidoscope? A kaleidoscope is a very fascinating instrument within which bits of colored glass, beads, stones, or other small pieces of materials are held loosely at the end of the tube. Mirrors set at angles in the tube as it is rotated reflect the materials, continuously changing patterns and designs as the loose colored pieces move about. Some artists have used this instrument to assist in creating colorful, new patterns of design. You could say that the mind works something like that in unraveling perplexities or generating new concepts.

There is a stage in the human thought process that has been documented again and again throughout history, and recorded by many, if not all, great men and women exceptional in the arts as well as in business and politics. It has been called an 'incubation' period by some.

Walter B. Canon, the American physiologist at the Harvard Medical School in the early 20th century who was known for discoveries related to bodily processes and the nervous system, had this to say, "As a matter of routine I have long trusted unconscious processes to serve me. . .for example, when I have had to prepare a public address. I would gather points for the

113

address and write them down in rough outline. Within the next few nights I would have sudden spells of awakening, with an onrush of illustrative instances, pertinent phrases and fresh ideas related to those already listed. The process has been so common and so reliable for me that I have supposed that it was at the service of everyone."

Jules-Henri Poincare, an eminent French scientist and a mathematician of the 19th century related this experience in pursuing a geometric problem in his writing 'Science et Methode:' ". . .but all my efforts were of no avail at first, except to make me better understand the difficulty, which is already something. All this work was perfectly conscious. Thereupon I left for Mont-Valerien, where I had to serve time in the army, and so my time was preoccupied with other matters. One day I was crossing the street, the solution of the difficulty which had brought me to standstill came to me all at once." This incident he referred to was his discoveries in his study of Fuchsian functions.

It was said that Thomas Alva Edison made it a practice to have several different problems in the process of solutions, and he switched from one problem to another whenever he reached a impasse of some kind. This permitted him, of course, to pause for the subconscious processing of information or mental pictures he had gathered.

Edgar Degas, the famous painter of ballet scenes, said he acquired the practice of just looking or doing a quick sketch of a subject; and, then later, working without a model or subject before him. His explanation, "It's a transformation in which your imagination collaborates with your memory."

Bertrand Russell, the noted English mathematician and philosopher, in his 'Portraits from Memory and Other Essays,' explained, "I have discovered ways of writing with a minimum of worry and anxiety. When I was young, each fresh piece of serious work used to seem to me for a time. . .perhaps too long a time. . .to be beyond my powers. I would fret myself into a nervous state from fear that it was never going to come right. I would make one unsatisfying attempt after another, and in the end have to discard them all. At last I found that such fumbling

114

attempts were a waste of time. It appeared that after first contemplating a book on some subject and after giving serious preliminary attention to it, I needed a period of subconscious incubation which could not be hurried and was, if anything, impeded by deliberate thinking. Sometimes I would find, after a time, that I had made a mistake, and that I could not write the book I had had in mind. But often I was more fortunate. Having by a time of intense concentration planted the problem in my subconsciousness, it would germinate underground until, suddenly, the solution emerged with blinding clarity, so that it only remained to write down what had appeared as if in a revelation."

This much referenced phenomenon is a time when everything is put aside, detachment of oneself from deliberation, away from the gathering of information, or abandoning the absorbing pursuit of an idea or a solution to a perplexing problem. After becoming so buried in the study of a subject or in an activity, lying back and relaxing, and breaking away into some other kind of activity, giving no further conscious thought to what has been pursued.

During this interlude the mind will process in its subconscious work all of the images, the information, the experiences stored there. Like the kaleidoscope, its processors form combinations out of the knowledge and images stored both consciously and unconsciously. . .sorting, matching concordant information, rejecting that which does not seem to fit until a perfect combination is achieved. Sorting the odds and ends of earlier experiences, study, images, reading, listening and observations from a conscious search for information.

In 'The Art of Scientific Investigation' by W.I.B. Beveridge, he noted from his studies, ". . .it was pointed out that ideas spring straight into the conscious mind without our having deliberately formed them. Evidently they originate from the subconscious activities of the mind which, when directed at a problem, immediately brings together various ideas which have been associated with that particular subject before. When a possible significant combination is found, it is presented to the conscious mind for its appraisal." Ideas and solutions to problems are derivatives of a deeper, totally unconscious field of influence and experience of which the conscious mind was never aware or even suspected.

All of the knowledge, visualizations, and memories lodged in those thousand upon thousands of independent modules in the subconscious mind performing their tasks along with the information consciously and freshly gathered turned this way and that. All of this combined into new forms and patterns by the subconscious mind's processors before presenting a practicable solution to the conscious mind. This kaleidoscopic activity would be happening right now as you are reading, though you may not be aware of its processing. It continues every hour of the day and every hour of the night.

We spend about a third of our lives asleep. The exact reason we must sleep is still not fully understood by science. Sleep has stumped psychiatrists. They have no idea what sleep does. What takes place then in the circuitry of our mind remains a big question mark. Could our dreams while sleeping also come from this process of sorting and comparing past experiences with the most recent?

Carl Gustave Jung said that, "The dream is the small hidden door in the deepest most intimate sanctum of the soul." Could it not be that for one brief moment in our deep sleep we are permitted to peek through the small hidden door to our subconscious mind revealing the brain processing, turning over and over a myriad of combinations of the images, the experiences, the memories consciously or unconsciously stored there in those minute modules? A strange procession of people, places, things, and events combined in many ways, imaged and voiced while we are deep in sleep.

Morton Prince, the American neurologist, said that in a dream-vision it was possible to trace the thoughts back to antecedent experiences of the dreamer, and he referred to a 'subconscious intelligence.' Here again it would be like the kaleidoscope changing and constructing new combinations; discerning and selecting, contrasting and comparing the collection of information and images stored for the solution of problems or ideas. This could be the mind's effort to make good sense out of the spontaneous, random collection of experiences it records; setting aside some and embracing others. Never believe that your dreams are not real. . .some of our dreams come true every day.

There is something that certainly everyone has experienced. You have gone to bed at night and fallen into a deep sleep. Upon arising in the morning you remember and possibly tell someone about the dream you've had. It could have been something of this nature. "It seemed I was playing in a schoolyard filled with kids. My childhood playmate, little Margie Brown, was with me. Her hair was done up in curls. She was dressed neatly as always. She wore a short, ruffled, dress-up dress with white anklets and bright shiny black shoes.

"All of a sudden across the schoolyard walked my Uncle George, grinning and shouting (though he died many years ago). Then the scene changed again. I was in a big house. . .didn't recognize it. It had a long open stairway going up from the kitchen and down into the vestibule. There were many people there. I don't remember ever seeing any of them before."

And so it may have happened, some events or images from the past in your dream. Some things recorded in memory consciously and some unconsciously. Some happenings you may have never been aware of experiencing. This subconscious human reflection and the mind's processing under the surface of awareness is most difficult to understand.

Many attested to knowing this process buried deep in our subconscious mind. Many have used the process solving problems and constructing new concepts. The Harvard physiologist suggested, *it is at the service of everyone.*

Creators of works of art, literary works, scientific investigators, and others in generations past as well as today have recorded their personal experience with this phenomenon. This has been an interruption by choice or by chance during the conscious pursuit of a difficult problem. It has happened during a period of intense work on a writing or painting. A long period of conscious, zealous effort without a satisfactory result. Then an illumination after a cessation or intermission for a time during which the problem was put aside for other conscious activity.

117

Many have used this pausal interlude when pursuing a knotty problem, searching for some new concept, while itching for a brilliant or beautiful musical phrase, or casting about for a certain expression or feeling in a painting. They have simply given it a rest, broke the ties with the activity in which they were engaged. It would be something as simple as going to bed and sleeping on it. No restriction on the period of time given to this pausal interlude. It might be an hour or so, days or months. In the experience of Mark Twain, a matter of years.

There are many accounts of famous thinkers, artists, musicians, writers, and people in various fields of science that have referred to this interlude or pause in the pursuit of an answer to a question or revelation leading to a wonderful creative product. They left their problem or search in care of their subconscious mind. Both awareness and intuition are the living powers and prime agents of all human perception. The conscious action and the subconscious reaction. They 'come with the territory,' but the method must be discovered by each person and be developed and nurtured before becoming a part of one's skills.

THE GOOD SENSE OF NONSENSE

From the moment I picked up your book until I laid it down, I was convulsed with laughter. Some day I intend reading it.

Groucho Marx *(to S. J. Perelman)*

A sense of humor, intelligence, and inventiveness are closely related. Humor will appear suddenly in the form of a smile, grin or laughter, and comes from the depths of the subconscious where lies the mind's creative processing. 'Bartlett's Familiar Quotations' and similar books, compilations of quotations from noted people and bits of wisdom from the past, include more than eighty percent of what could be called witticisms.

Laughter comes from experiencing the unexpected. These are the reverses that trick you by a switch in point of view. A story or account of an event that is going one way and, at the last minute, goes another way and catches us by surprise. An analogy with a switch in direction, or an imitation of someone or something for comic effect or ridicule. An exaggeration of a common situation or description of something or someone. Equivocation in using a word with two unexpected or ribald meanings. Any of these will result in laughter when the audience, whoever it may be, is pleasantly surprised.

Wit in writing or in art, or in a performance on stage can be amusingly clever in expression. It can be original in its communication to its audience. Both serious and humorous prose are carefully scripted, rehearsed, edited, and rewritten to gain a planned reaction, as is a professional comic's material. A planned reaction of surprise that might not be revealed or expected until the last word or phrase has been delivered.

This is not unlike the wonder or off-guard reaction whenever the mind unlocks its secrets and displays its subconscious contents. When elation and surprise come with the sudden and unexplained discovery of a solution to a stubborn problem or in the gaining of some special aspiration. The abrupt arrival of a mind's revelation, a discovery, or conceptualization is also unpredictable, coming when least expected.

Those who have created something original and exciting. . .a work of art, a writing of some importance, a musician's or an actor's performance, a scientific discovery of merit. . .often will look with wonder upon that which they created. I have heard artists when completing an especially nice work say, "it was so easy as though something or someone else was guiding my hand while I stood back and watched." I have talked to writers who have said that they reread their completed work with disbelief that they themselves could have written a piece so brilliantly. This again was the unseen and unpredictable work of the subconscious mind surfacing in an unexpected burst of exhilaration. Some describe as an 'illumination' this happy, fulfilling accident that happens when our subconscious processing reveals to our conscious minds unexpectedly the unraveling of a knotty problem or clarification of a puzzling definition, proposition or concept. It will leave the person who experiences this with a feeling they had no part in it.

Albert Einstein said with sincerity, "I know quite certainly that I myself have no special talent. Curiosity, obsession and dogged endurance, combined with self-criticism, have brought me to my ideas. Especially strong thinking powers I do not have, or only to a modest degree. Many have far more of those than I without producing anything surprising."

We often dismiss or overlook how the mind in its subconscious work has thrown light upon a seemingly insoluble search for an answer to a problem or assisted in the completion of some type of effort. The unplanned and unexpected response to a search for information, a scheme or program for making, doing, or arranging something. The mind performing unconsciously that which the conscious mind does not or cannot succeed in doing.

Many accidental and unexpected breakthroughs in the sciences have been recorded throughout history. Such happenstances, when they were recognized as important by someone with expertise in the particular field, resulted in a strikingly important advance or discovery for the treatment of some diseases. Such was the discovery of the therapeutic use of penicillin and sulfanilamide. Also, those with so much societal impact by Alexander Graham Bell, the telephone, and the beginning of electronics by William C. Roentgen's discovery of X-rays.

These accidental discoveries actually were possible because of minds consciously committed to research and study in a particular field. In exploring and building experience in allied subjects they recognized in their experimentation the significance of some pattern or combination of ideas suggested by their innermost accumulation of information. The subconscious processing and rummaging through their store of data to suggest steps in trial and testing.

Note that the appellation 'discovery' is more fitting than the descriptive word 'invention.' We cannot in any way invent an element that is not already of our universe. We can only discover applications of the elements in our present world in ways and methods new to we humans. We can only take what we have and discover new ways of using it.

Of course, all revelations from the depths of the subconscious are not earthshaking explosions of new information. The answers to an overriding, complex question often come from a series of solutions to germane subjects of investigation. A progressive, deliberate opening of doors one after another to new levels of clarification. Slogging on until the core of the original query is solved or discovered.

Thomas Alva Edison wrote down every new idea that he came upon regardless of how important or unimportant it might have seemed at the moment. He looked upon these as preliminary breakthroughs, steps to new levels of discovery that could lead to something of major importance.

The sudden unveiling of a discovery or idea and the exhilaration that follows without any constraint, effort, or premeditation is much the same as the off-guard reaction to a comedian's wit, the surprise ending of a joke or quip. Jules-Henri Poincare, the French mathematician, wrote, "One is at once struck by these appearances of sudden illumination, obvious indications of a long course of previous unconscious

121

work." And, always with the warm feeling and comfort of the attainment of one's purpose.

Some have said that such illuminations have come in the morning after a good night's sleep. For others, a flash of insight during a quiet walk in the fresh air of the evening, or a period of relaxation while the mind is not otherwise occupied. Or suddenly when in a conversation with someone related to a pursued problem the answer is released.

It is interesting that an automatic, subconscious reaction to some kind of stimulus can result in spontaneous laughter. We do not have conscious control over it. We can put ourselves into situations conducive to laughter, or be in a good mood for laughter with a happy, open disposition for comedy. But, we do not make it happen naturally (though a good actor can feign laughter). The reaction is directed by the unconscious mind. . .a subconscious response to a surprising action or proposition.

We will laugh at an unexpected success or accidental discovery. It is possible sometimes to suppress the onset of laughter with great difficulty. A burst of laughter that socially must be suppressed can emerge when our subconscious is taken unawares by something unsuitable or inappropriate. Some will suppress a smile or laughter when the timing of humor is in conflict with their social or political stance. But chance discoveries or surprises are most always worthy of a satisfying, subconscious explosion of glee. It soothes one and relaxes. It is a happy, welcome transfusion of passion for the human soul.

PERFECTION IN KNOWLEDGE AND SKILLS
...YOUR CHOICE... RECOGNITION
...THE CHOICE OF OTHERS

Genius is only recognized in people who succeed.
William Merrit Chase,
American Impressionist

It is unfortunate that the label, 'genius,' is only given to someone by popular acclaim in their time. For example, the paintings of Johannes Vermeer, the Dutch painter of the 17th century, had a powerfully constructed design of interiors that were his alone. Yet his light was more or less obscured, and his works were often ascribed to more popular artists of the time. As a result, only 35 of his paintings have survived, rediscovered little more than a century ago. Rembrandt on the other hand, prolific in his many works that continue to live on, was so popular in his day that works of contemporaries were often purported to have been painted by him.

Of course, there are many ordinary people who become highly skilled, keen of mind, creatively professional. Many of these toil away in the obscurity of a business office, a studio, or their home performing masterly without any kind of public notice. Their achievements, not considered earthshaking by the public, may only be significant to some small group within a limited field of interests. These may be important only to those in the same occupation or activity, and they only receive their reward for what they have accomplished through the comfort of their victory.

Many people solve imposing problems every day with wisdom and alacrity. For most of us it takes a lot of prudence and originality just to get through a day. Solving the problems of crossing the street without getting hit by a car, how to get the house in order and dinner ready before company arrives. Truly inventive can be the unpresuming housewife who plans an evening meal with a bit of a flair. Or a husband who suddenly presents his wife with a surprising, treasured gift out of his heart.

If our only definition of someone of genius is Charlotte Bronte at a desk penning 'Jane Eyre,' or Michelangelo at work painting frescos in the Sistine Chapel, we should take a more mundane perspective. I would not wish to reduce to a triviality things so wonderful and important as the achievements of the most celebrated creators of art, sculpture, or literature. My message is that many people near to us are trained and labor creatively and successfully at some kind of important activity. Important to only a few others who have a common affinity, but nevertheless of import to the lives of others.

Anyone who reaches a goal or fulfills their potential in anything, who strikes out with the intent and drive to succeed at something, demonstrates intelligence and vision. Many great concepts that have contributed to the betterment of our lives and modes of living have come from unlikely sources. Their discoveries probably made while they were pursuing their day-to-day vocations. These achievements were no less important to us than those of the famous achievers in the past. Everyone has a potential for a great performance or accomplishment given the right books to read, the informed people to speak to, and the right paths to follow.

During the classic age artists, poets, composers, or philosophers lived within a smaller population. Their popularity among their contemporaries brought them their glorification. Those who then gained fame and success most often came from wealth or situations in their lives that permitted them to spend all of their time at their chosen craft. They were without the concern usually of searching for the means of providing food and lodging for themselves and their families.

Living in a world that patronized the arts above all else, little wonder that their efforts were recorded in history. If the classic master painter Edgar Degas was alive today, who knows but that he might be working in the offices of Saks Fifth Avenue in their advertising department as a commercial artist.

A general notion is that intelligence and 'talent' come only to certain people who were gifted at birth with their skill. Something inherited in some way along with the color of their eyes, hair, or skin, the size of their ears or the shape of their nose. We have been led to believe that there are few truly intelligent and inventive people in our world, and that we in the madding crowd must simply be satisfied with our lot and accept their works and direction to provide for our personal needs.

A Japanese gentleman died recently at the age of 99. His name, not widely recognized, was Shinichi Suzuki, the son of a violin manufacturer. After advanced studies on the violin in Germany, he went on later to join the faculty of the Imperial Musical School in Tokyo, Japan. He also taught at their Kunitachi College of Music. He believed that 'talent' was learned rather than inherited; and, with the right training, anyone could master music. He had a motto: "A talent is not something given naturally; it is something you foster."

Shinichi pioneered a method for teaching toddlers to play musical instruments the same way that they learn to speak. . .by early and constant exposure. His 'mother tongue method,' as he preferred to call it, was his realization that any child who can learn to speak a language, can learn to play music by age three by listening and imitation.

He introduced his method and formed the Suzuki Talent Education Research Institute in the 1950s. He took his method conceived for the violin to the United States as the Suzuki Association of the Americas, expanding his instruction method to the piano and all musical instruments.

Since the introduction of his Suzuki teaching method, hundreds of thousands of young musicians have been trained to perform remarkably in this way. More than 300,000 children in 34 countries are learning music successfully by the Suzuki method, two-thirds of them in the United States. . .by exposure to music, by listening, by imitation.

Shinichi believed that each child "must be educated with infinite care." He said, "I want to make good citizens, noble human beings. It is in our power to educate all children of the world to become a little better as people, a little happier."

Shinichi did not believe the presumption that we are capable of knowing something beyond what we see with our eyes or hear with our ears. He questioned that there could be some kind of knowledge other than that which is strictly empirical. And, proved this again and again through his own successful teaching of children.

Pinchas Zukerman, violin virtuoso Music Director of the National Arts Centre Orchestra of Canada, Music Director of the Ilona Feher Music Center in Holom, Israel, and chair of the Pinchas Zukerman Performance Program at the Manhattan School of Music, professed, "There is no such thing as a person born without any musical talent. The music is inside of us. We just have to know how to bring it out."

Children are eager to learn and do search for someone they can look up to and respect. Those held in awe by the public today are not the best role models for the children. The media have focused our attention upon sexual deviates, drug users, felons, rapists, and murderers, which they exploit and the public views with wonder. Is it really a better, the more popular way to lead their lives by imitating this immoral, tawdry, tinsel element in action, dress, and mindset?

Countless girls and boys in our country have been sexually molested before they have reached 18 years of age. And, as studies have shown, they more likely were abused by relatives or acquaintances. Their legacy is to develop a behavior that is hostile to social order or antagonistic to the principles by which society is guided. This can undoubtedly emerge in sexually explicit conduct, homosexuality or lesbianism, prostitution, isolation from society and deep depression. The way a person acts from the standpoint of morality and ethics is not caused by genetic effect or physical chemistry, but by the imperfect relationships and experiences in life.

We can see everywhere the magnificent forms of human, plant, and animal life that populate and beautify this earth we live upon. But, try looking about a crowded bus during the rush hour, and see how much of the bared human appears in all of the faces there. Defensive signs or excuse, if not pleasure and peace. So very controversial are the attempts by science to explain causal agents of the many ills in our society, because there is so much still to learn and understand about the roots of behavior.

Why do so many people hate each other? Why to people become amoral?

So many conflicts are hidden within human behavior. A revealing picture will come from consideration of the cultural and environmental differences, interfamily or intersocial relationships. How can we help counter violence and the other immoral pitfalls that prevent children from becoming productive and innocent society serving adults? Whence came the easy, indifferent attitude toward virtue that today has become part of our culture and is influencing our moral judgments? And, the unending, futile and gainless genetic search for life's origin?

To paraphrase a statement by the Bishop Raymondo J. Pena of Brownsville, Texas. . .when it is all said and done, we must simply take a deep breath and admit somehow, without our willing it, we are here and alive. We each have come into existence with very little understanding of what we observe and can describe in our human bodies. The design is intricate, subtle, harmonius, and we are walking miracles. The gift of life is ours to possess without cost, ours to cherish, to nurture, to protect, to celebrate, and to reverence.

-- THE END --